D1716740

EXPLORING THE ANCIENT
AND MEDIEVAL WORLDS

Asia Through the Ages
Early History to European Colonialism

Patricia Dawson

Cavendish
Square

New York

Published in 2016 by Cavendish Square Publishing, LLC
243 5th Avenue, Suite 136, New York, NY 10016

Copyright © 2016 by Cavendish Square Publishing, LLC

First Edition

Website: cavendishsq.com

This publication represents the opinions and views of the author based on his or her personal experience, knowledge, and
research. The information in this book serves as a general guide only. The author and publisher have used their best efforts
in preparing this book and disclaim liability rising directly or indirectly from the use and application of this book.

CPSIA Compliance Information: Batch #WS15CSQ

All websites were available and accurate when this book was sent to press.

Cataloging-in-Publication Data

Dawson, Patricia.
Asia through the ages: early history to european colonialism / by Patricia Dawson.
p. cm. — (Exploring the ancient and medieval worlds)
Includes index.
ISBN 978-1-50260-683-9 (hardcover) ISBN 978-1-50260-684-6 (ebook)
1. Asia — History — Juvenile literature. 2. Colonies — Asia — Juvenile literature.
3. Asia — Civilization — Juvenile literature. I. Dawson, Patricia. II. Title.
DS33.5 D39 2016
950—d23

Editorial Director: David McNamara
Editor: Nathan Heidelberger
Copy Editor: Regina Murrell
Art Director: Jeff Talbot
Designer: Joseph Macri
Senior Production Manager: Jennifer Ryder-Talbot
Production Editor: Renni Johnson
Photo Research: J8 Media

Printed in the United States of America

Contents

Chapter 1: Early Chinese History   5

Chapter 2: Philosophy in Ancient China   19

Chapter 3: China's Growing Empire   33

Chapter 4: The History of Japan   47

Chapter 5: The First Civilizations of India   61

Chapter 6: The Rise of Hinduism   77

Chapter 7: The Buddha and His Teachings   91

Chapter 8: India's History Continues   107

Chapter 9: Cultures of Southeast Asia   121

Chapter 10: Pacific Island Cultures   133

Chronology   142
Glossary   146
Major Historical Figures   151
For Further Information   153
Index   154

This modern reconstruction, based on the remains of Peking Man, shows what *Homo erectus* may have looked like.

CHAPTER ONE

Early Chinese History

At the dawn of recorded history, China did not exist as a single, unified entity. Instead, a number of separate early human cultures emerged independently of each other, spread throughout the region. While they began to come together at around 2200 BCE, it wasn't until 221 BCE that the first emperor officially joined them into one kingdom.

The first people appeared in China around two million years ago. Known as *Homo erectus*, they were the ancestors of modern humans. It is uncertain whether *Homo erectus* originated in Africa and spread out around the world or whether the earliest humans developed independently in Africa and Asia. *Homo erectus* had a smaller brain than the modern human, but differed from the ape by walking upright rather than on all fours. *Homo erectus* was the first humanoid species to use fire and to live in caves.

The *Homo erectus* remains that were found in 1927 CE in caves at Zhoukoudian became known as Peking Man—after the former English name for the nearest city, Beijing. The remains, dated to around 460,000 years ago, show that Peking Man used implements made of rock and animal bones, hunted and ate animals, and lived communally in caves.

From Hunting to Farming

For many thousands of years, early humans lived in China as hunter-gatherers. The *Homo erectus* species was gradually superseded with a wealthy aristocracy and rule by a hereditary monarch. Most of the people were poor farmers who grew millet, wheat, barley, and rice, as well as raised sheep, oxen, pigs, and dogs. The rulers appointed by the king were the masters of the farms, the landed estates, and the villages surrounding the cities. The elite had access to bronze objects and placed them in their graves (see sidebar, page 11), but the majority still lived as their ancestors had lived in the Stone Age, using wooden spades and stone sickles. The poor people's earthenware was rough, while their masters' was delicate and ornate.

A literate priestly class was responsible for matters of religion. The priests' main duties were to divine the future by interpreting bone oracles and to channel advice from a panel of deities headed by Shang Di (Shang Ti; the Lord on High). The Shang people worshipped their ancestors as well as their gods, sacrificing both humans and animals to them. The priests were also expected to keep records. Tens of thousands of oracular writings of the period have been preserved, and it is because of those records that so much more is known about the late Shang period (ca. 1250–1050 BCE) than about the earlier Shang period.

The divination records are the oldest texts in the Chinese language. Chinese writing uses a single character for every word, and there are more than forty thousand characters altogether. Some three thousand characters from the Shang dynasty have been identified, incised on tortoiseshells and on the scapulae (shoulder blades) of the cattle and sheep that were used as oracles in divination ceremonies. Around eight hundred of them have been deciphered with certainty. Chinese writing has since undergone many changes, but its basic structure and many of its symbols remain unaltered.

The Zhou Dynasty

According to traditional accounts, the **Zhou (Chou)** took control of China around 1050 BCE and subjugated the Shang. The Zhou lived in the valley of the Wei River in the far west of China. They belonged to a different ethnic group from the Shang, although they shared the same bronze culture. The traditional Chinese account describes the last Shang king as a degenerate monster whose replacement by the Zhou was the will of heaven; the Shang's divine mandate to rule had been

The Xinjiang Mummies and the Uyghurs

More than one hundred naturally preserved bodies, dating from as long ago as 2000 BCE, have been found in the Xinjiang region of northwestern China. The corpses, the first of which was discovered in 1978 CE, had avoided decomposition through burial in the hot, dusty soil between the Celestial Mountains (Tian Shan) and the Taklimakan Desert.

Museumgoers examine the remains of one of the Xinjiang mummies.

The mummies have Caucasian rather than Asiatic facial features, dark-brown or yellow-blond hair, and long limbs. They were all buried with patterned woven cloth, and some graves contained wagon wheels. Made of three carved boards fastened with dowels, the wheels are virtually identical to wheels made in Ukraine, on the plains of eastern Europe. The people were seemingly either travelers from Europe or the descendants of Europeans.

Scholars have debated the significance of the finds. Some historians suggest that the bodies are the remains of raiders or nomads; others contend that Caucasian people were actually typical of the population in the area at the time (ca. 2000–1000 BCE) and that East Asian peoples arrived there only after around 1000 BCE. Some ancient Chinese texts describe encounters with tall blond people; scholars had previously dismissed such accounts as imaginary, but the Xinjiang mummies compelled them to reconsider.

Today, most inhabitants of the area are Uyghurs, a Turkic people who are also resident in several of the states that border modern China, notably Kazakhstan, Kyrgyzstan, and Pakistan, as well as in Uzbekistan. Some Uyghurs want to establish an independent state of their own, East Turkestan (also known as Uyghurstan).

passed on to the Zhou. The same justification for the seizure of power had previously been used to legitimize the Shang replacement of the Xia. Thereafter, such explanations became standard every time there was a change of dynasty.

The Zhou ruled most of northern China, including the fertile banks of the Yangtze River. Their domain was so extensive and communication so limited that they delegated administrative tasks to hereditary vassals. Each lord ruled over designated territory that he controlled with his own army. Agricultural lands were divided into squares of nine plots; peasant families worked the outer eight tracts as their own land and collectively farmed the central tract for their lord. Below peasants in the social order were domestic slaves.

The lords in each state were nominally subordinate to the dynastic king, who was said to rule by mandate from heaven, but in reality the lords became more powerful than the king. They frequently warred with each other, and the victors seized the territory of the vanquished. Through a process of consolidation, the states became larger, fewer in number, and increasingly autonomous, forcing the king to share power with the lords. Eventually, the king was no more than a figurehead.

On the periphery of China, states formed alliances with non-Chinese groups. In 770 BCE, an alliance of several states and non-Chinese forces drove the Zhou to establish a new capital in the east at Loyang. The rulers from this period are thus known as the Eastern Zhou. They had little control over their dependent states.

During this period, the chariot—long central to the conduct of battle—was replaced by infantry as the main instrument of war. Farmers were forced to serve in the infantry and came under increasingly direct control even when they were not mobilized.

From the fifth century BCE, a regular army became essential to China as the country was called on to resist repeat incursions from the north and west. The frequency of the attacks increased greatly in the fourth century BCE, when nomads from the steppes of central Asia attacked Chinese farmers time and again. In an effort to defend the Chinese people against such raids, the rulers of the Zhou era built long walls, usually of clay, along their northern and western frontiers. They also erected defensive walls between the various states.

Excavating the City of Yin

The late Shang capital of Yin (Yinxu) at modern Anyang in Henan Province was excavated between 1927 and 1936 CE. Yin was a major city that, at its peak around 1250–1050 BCE, extended for 3.6 miles (5.8 kilometers) along the Huan River and included a wealth of palaces, temples, and royal graves.

All but one of the royal graves of Yin had been plundered. The exception was the tomb of Fu Hao, queen of the twenty-first Shang king, Wu Ding (Wu Ting; ruled 1250–1192 BCE). Her grave was found to contain more than 3,500 pounds (1,600 kilograms) of bronze pieces; around six hundred items of carved stone, jade, and bone; nearly seven thousand cowrie shells (then used as currency); sixteen human skeletons (presumably attendants); and six dog skeletons.

This oracle bone from the ancient city of Yin features one of the earliest examples of written Chinese.

Other graves at Anyang contained evidence of similarly grand burials, including mass interments of people and animals (monkeys, deer, horses, and even elephants) and the oldest chariots in China. The bronze vessels in the Anyang graves originally contained offerings of food and wine for the spirits of ancestors. In addition, the graves included a collection of oracle bones, which are of particular importance because, during the Shang dynasty, the questions posed by diviners and the answers received from heaven were recorded for the first time on the bones, making them a form of early historical text. Before the Anyang finds, Chinese script was thought to have developed from Sumerian and ancient Egyptian writing, but it is now known to have evolved independently.

The states made alliances with each other against the invaders. Such treaties among the individual states provided them with the political stability that they needed as the power of the Zhou dynasty began to wane during the seventh and sixth centuries BCE. However, by the late fifth century BCE, most of the alliances among the states had failed. The era of civil conflict and anarchy that ensued—known as the **Period of the Warring States** (ca. 475–221 BCE)—overlaps with the final centuries of the Zhou dynasty, which continued as the ruling dynasty until its collapse in 256 BCE.

The late Zhou period was a time of enormous significance in Chinese economic and political development. Despite the conflict and unrest, the era was prosperous. The Bronze Age gave way to the Iron Age, as iron tools and weapons, first introduced into China around 500 BCE, became commonplace. A market economy emerged that was based on coins. China's first laws were written. An administrative system was set up that allowed the government to undertake large-scale public works such as the construction of river dykes, irrigation systems, and canals. The population expanded as farming became significantly more productive, largely as a result of vast irrigation projects.

However, despite the new prosperity, life remained very hard for many people. Farmers were still often victims of war, whether as soldiers or noncombatants, and had to pay exorbitant taxes; epidemics, floods, and famine still brought periodic devastation. Many farmers, having fallen on hard times, were forced to sell their children in order to survive or had to accept work as laborers on grand projects such as an ostentatious grave for a member of the aristocracy.

The final years of the Zhou dynasty also saw an extraordinary flowering of philosophy in China. The two main stimuli were **Confucius (Konqui)** and **Lao-tzu (Laozi)**, sixth-century BCE thinkers whose teachings gave rise to the philosophical and religious programs of **Confucianism** and **Taoism (Daoism)**.

Shi Huang Di, the First Emperor

In 221 BCE, the northwestern feudal state of Qin (Ch'in), which was richer and militarily stronger than its neighbors, seized the royal power that the Chinese states had warred over since 500 BCE. The king of

Qin, influenced by the work of the philosopher Shang Yang (ca. 390–338 BCE), declared himself **Shi Huang Di (Shi Huang Ti)**, or first emperor of the **Qin dynasty**. The Chinese called their country either by the name of its current ruling dynasty or Zhongguot (Chung-kuo; the Middle Kingdom), which reflected their perception of themselves as being at the center of the world. Eventually, the name China—a variation of Qin—was adopted by the rest of the world as the permanent name of the country, regardless of its ruler.

The Qin regime adopted the philosophy of legalism, one of the fundamental tenets of which was that people are naturally evil and therefore need to be ruled by a strong king, army, and administration. The first emperor of China imposed a centralized administration on the semiautonomous feudal states that had existed before his accession. He broke up the lands of aristocratic families into provinces and assigned bureaucrats to run them. He encouraged private landholding, and those who received the land as private property became members of the privileged classes. They controlled the system of taxation and lobbied for influence at court. Meanwhile, the situation of the average farmer did not improve much.

Work on the Great Wall of China began under the Qin regime. Later dynasties would continue to extend and improve this monumental feat of engineering.

The first emperor built the **Great Wall of China**, which combined long stretches of preexisting defensive walls into a single, vast, continuous barrier. During the course of his reign, the emperor added around 1,200 miles (1,930 km) to the frontier defenses. When the wall was completed in 204 BCE, it extended for 4,160 miles (6,700 km) along the country's northern and eastern frontiers. The use of forced labor to achieve this construction feat later became a popular cause of resentment.

In addition, the first emperor ruthlessly expanded his territory. He forced peasants into military service and dispatched his armies south to the Yuan Hong (Yüan Hung; the Red River in modern Vietnam). He took control of the enormous area covered by the modern provinces of Sichuan (Szechwan), Yunnan (Yün-nan), and Guizhou (Kuei-chou), as well as all of China north of the Yangtze River, including parts of the Korean Peninsula. Under Shi Huang Di, the Qin regime promoted economic and social integration across this vast empire, imposing standardized coinage, weights, measures, and culture. Shi Huang Di also simplified written Chinese. He tried to impose the philosophy of legalism on all his domains, and in 213 BCE, he ordered the infamous burning of the books, in which all written documents except works of history, divination, agriculture, and medicine were cast into the flames. He tolerated no opposition, even in philosophy; no fewer than 460 scholars were executed during his reign.

The first emperor was also obsessed with the idea of an elixir that could bring eternal youth. In 219 BCE, following the guidance of his diviners, he sent three thousand of his young subjects on a mission across the Eastern Sea in search of a legendary Land of the Immortals. None of the explorers returned. Many years later, legends arose suggesting that the lost youths had discovered the islands of Japan and settled there.

The authority and the organizational skills of the first emperor are apparent in his vast burial mound near the modern city of Xi'an. The earthworks at the site measure around one-third of a mile (500 meters) in diameter. Inside them was an underground reconstruction of China, including re-creations of the Yangtze River, the Yellow River, and the starry heavens dotted with pearls. In 1974 CE, while digging a water well around 1,000 yards (1 km) to the east of the tomb, local farmers

The Long River

China's Yangtze River is the longest natural waterway in Asia, flowing 3,400 miles (5,470 km) from the Kunlun Mountains in southwest Qinghai (Tsinghai) Province, south through Sichuan (Szechwan) Province into Yunnan (Yün-nan) Province, then northeast and east across central China to the East China Sea, just north of Shanghai. The Chinese name for the river is Chang Jiang (Ch'ang Chiang), meaning "Long River"; within China, the name Yangtze technically

The Yangtze River, Asia's longest, is essential to Chinese agriculture.

refers only to the last 400 miles (644 km) of the river's course, where it flows through the region of the tenth-century BCE Yang kingdom.

The river drains more than 650,000 square miles (1,683,500 square kilometers) of China through its numerous tributaries. Its main branches are the Han, the Yalong (Ya-lung), the Jialing (Chia-ling), the Min, the Tuo He (T'o Ho), the Wu, and the Huang He (Huang Ho; Yellow River).

The regions around China's great rivers are the most populous and economically productive areas of the country. The Yangtze is navigable by seagoing ships for 600 miles (965 km) from its mouth and by river steamers for 1,000 miles (1,609 km), but passage through the Yangtze Gorges is perilous for boats. With its tributaries, the river is a great fertilizer of the land. Chinese civilization, based on agriculture, originated in the great river valleys. The Huang He derives its English name from the large quantity of yellow clay it carries. This clay or silt is known as *loess*, a fertile loam, and each flooding of the river leaves a layer of loess on the land, greatly increasing its fertility. The Yangtze deposits more than 6 billion cubic feet (168 million cubic meters) of silt annually in Jiangsu Province alone, helping the region to be a major producer of rice.

discovered four pits containing a buried terra-cotta army, comprising more than eight thousand life-sized statues of soldiers with their horses. The figures were arrayed in military formation, ready to defend the emperor in the afterlife.

The Han Dynasty Takes Over

The reign of the Qin empire's founding family was short-lived— just fifteen years. Several popular uprisings followed on the heels of the first emperor's death in 210 BCE, an indication, perhaps, of the unpopularity of the Qin's legalist philosophy. In 206 BCE, a nonaristocratic army officer, **Liu Bang (Liu Pang)**, declared the end of the rebellion and the advent of the new **Han dynasty.** The Hans ruled for over four centuries, until 220 CE. While they held on to the Qin's centralized administrative system, the Han emperors abandoned most of the tenets of legalism. Instead, they eventually opted to organize the governance of their vast domain around the principles of Confucianism.

China's iconic terra-cotta warriors were built to guard the tomb of Qin Shi Huang Di, the country's first emperor.

A contemporary monument to Confucius, one of the ancient world's most influential philosophers

CHAPTER TWO

Philosophy in Ancient China

Confucius and Lao-tzu, China's two greatest philosophers, were both born in the sixth century BCE. The teachings of these two thinkers have been widely studied throughout southern and eastern Asia and beyond. They have left a lasting mark on Chinese history and culture.

The late years of the Zhou (Chou) dynasty, between the sixth and the third centuries BCE, saw an extraordinary flowering of philosophy in China that would eventually exert a significant and lasting influence on China's neighbors throughout eastern Asia. By 480 BCE, the Zhou rulers, whose ancestors had governed since around 1050 BCE and had once held sway over a large part of China, no longer retained any real power. The country was politically fragmented, with several independent states competing for preeminence. Constant warfare, with its attendant confusion and insecurity, fostered a search for peace and order. Many Chinese people whose worldly ambitions had been thwarted sought consolation in ideas and theories.

During this period, a number of philosophical schools formulated new ideas about individual behavior and society. The most important such school was based on the teachings of Confucius. The philosophy that later became known in English as Confucianism would ultimately become the predominant tradition throughout China, Korea, Japan, and the northern part of Southeast Asia. The nine principal books of classical Chinese philosophy were all written during this period (see sidebar, page 23). In Chinese script, the character that means "classic"

Confucius and the Confucian philosophy inspired and codified a new concept of nobility. Previously in China, nobility had been regarded as an inborn characteristic of aristocrats only. However, for Confucius, nobility was a quality of soul that could be acquired by study, by honesty, and by living a virtuous life. He emphasized that it was possible for individuals to improve themselves and their society by cultivating their personal lives. By making such efforts, anyone could become a great sage. It followed that people should be promoted to government jobs on the basis of their ability rather than because of their birth or social standing.

Confucius attributed the misery of the warfare that was endemic in his time to a lack of nobility on the part of the rulers. He wrote: "When the personal life is cultivated, the family will be regulated; when the family is regulated, the state will be in order; and when the state is in order, there will be peace throughout the world."

Confucius's thinking was original in its rationalism and humanism. He did not deny the existence of the supernatural but believed that an appeal to it made no sense. The primary focus, he contended, should be on individual effort. His emphasis on secular human ethics was a new ideal for Chinese civilization.

Lao-tzu and the *Tao Te Ching*

Confucius's contemporary, Lao-tzu (Laozi), sought the Tao (the Dao; the Way; the supreme principle) in nature rather than in society. Very little is known of Lao-tzu's life. According to the *Shi-ji* (*Shih-chi*; *Records of the Grand Historian*)—written around 100 BCE by China's first historian, Sima Qian (Ssu-ma Ch'ien)—Lao-tzu was born around 570 BCE in what is now Hunan Province and served as an astrologer and fortune-teller at the royal Zhou court. However, many scholars doubt this biography (see sidebar, pages 26–27). Lao-tzu probably died around 490 BCE. From his teachings, it is clear that he examined nature to understand humanity and focused on personal growth through cultivation of inner calm and a pure mind.

The *Tao Te Ching* (*Dao De Jing*; *Classic of the Way and Its Virtue*), which explains this philosophy, is traditionally attributed to Lao-tzu

The *Wu Jing* and *Si Shu*

The **Wu Jing** (**Wu Ching**; **Five Classics**) are five texts dated to the Zhou (Chou) dynasty (ca. 600–500 BCE). According to tradition, they were edited or written by Confucius himself. The *I Ching* (*Yi Jing*; *Book of Changes*) is a divination manual. The *Shi Jing* (*Shih Ching*; *Classic of Poetry*) is a collection of 305 court songs, hymns, and folk songs. The *Li Ji* (*Li Chi*; *Classic of Rites*) is a manual of court ceremonies and social behavior. The *Shu Jing* (*Shu*

These coins, signifying luck, are used for divination in conjunction with the *I Ching*.

Ching; *Classic of History*) is a collection of documents reputedly written by early Zhou rulers. The *Lin Jing* (*Chun Qiu*; *Spring and Autumn Annals*) is a history of Confucius's native state of Lu from 722 to 479 BCE.

The *Si Shu* (*Ssu Shu*; *Four Books*) are four Confucian texts from the same period that were published in a single volume in 1190 CE (around 1,700 years after Confucius's lifetime) by the celebrated neo-Confucian scholar Chu Hsi. The first book is *Da Xue* (*Ta Hsüeh*; *Great Learning*), which gives an account of the links between a ruler's personal integrity and good government. The second is *Zong Yong* (*Chung Yung*; *The Doctrine of the Mean*), which investigates spiritual beings and the Tao. The third is the *Lun Yu* (*The Sayings of Confucius*), which supposedly contains direct quotations from Confucius recorded by his students. The last is the *Meng Zi* (*Meng-tzu*; *Mencius*), a record of the teachings of the Confucian disciple and scholar **Mencius** (ca. 371–289 BCE). Both *Great Learning* and *The Doctrine of the Mean* are also part of one of the *Five Classics*—*Classic of Rites*.

Chinese students are introduced to Confucian literature by studying the *Four Books*, which were the basis of Chinese civil service entrance examinations for almost six centuries, from 1313 to 1905 CE. More advanced students proceed to study the *Five Classics*.

This portrait of Lao-tzu, the founder of Taoism, was created by a medieval Chinese artist.

but was probably recorded by his students from the things he said. The book advises people to cultivate wu wei (nonaction), meaning that they should allow the Way to take its course. The book says: "Do nothing and all things are done." The ideal form of action, according to Lao-tzu, is not to try to think and do what is right, but to try to think and do nothing—what he calls the "doing of non-doing."

Lao-tzu emphasized a return to the simple agrarian life, a life not regulated by government. He urged rulers and government officials to avoid getting too involved in the trappings of power and in their actions: "When someone wishes to rule the world, he must be detached, because if he is drawn to object he will be unfit to rule the world."

Lao-tzu was aware that his teaching was difficult for some people to grasp. The *Tao Te Ching* states: "When the best kind of people learn the Way, then they are able, with dedication, to put it into practice. When average people are told of the Way, they can retain some things, but they forget the others. When the lowest kind of people hear of the Way, they laugh loudly at it. If they do not laugh at it, then it cannot be the Way."

Nonaction needed to be cultivated in allowing the Way to flow and in trusting it to find the right course, for it could be difficult to understand where the Way was leading. As the *Tao Te Ching* puts it: "The light Way seems dark; the Way that leads forward seems to lead backward."

The teachings of Lao-tzu are referred to as Taoism (Daoism). Following Lao-tzu's advice, many Taoists (Daoists) withdrew from active life to rural retreats, where they cultivated mental tranquility and tried to find wisdom; their aim, ultimately, was to have a mystical experience of nature that would bring them into harmony with the Way.

The ideals of Taoism were in opposition to the teachings of Confucianism. Where Confucianism offered guidance on how to live well in society and how to behave ethically, Taoism appeared to advocate withdrawal from society, even from activity. In contrast to the Confucians, followers of Taoism did not believe in the effectiveness of study: "Those who study hard increase every day. Those who have understood the Way decrease every day. They decrease and decrease until they reach the point where they do nothing."

However, following the Tao is not equivalent to idleness. As the *Tao Te Ching* notes of those who have understood the Way: "They do nothing and yet nothing remains undone." As the book also states, "Only the Way is good in beginning things and good in bringing things to an end." The emphasis of the two philosophies is notably different; the Tao of Taoism is a metaphysical-individualistic concept, whereas the Tao of Confucianism offers the ideal of correct behavior in a social context.

After Confucius

Subsequent philosophers expanded and developed the teachings of Confucius and Lao-tzu. The most important later Confucian thinker was Mengzi (Meng-tzu; ca. 371–289 BCE), who is known in the West as Mencius, the Latin form of his name.

Mencius advocated humane government. In a time when rulers were believed to be granted their positions by the mandate of heaven, Mencius emphasized the duty of the ruler to the people and insisted that government be exercised on behalf of the people.

Mencius, seen here, was an important later proponent of Confucianism.

This eighteenth-century CE Chinese ceramic depicts Lao-tzu seated upon a water buffalo. The philosopher allegedly rode a water buffalo out of the country when he became fed up with Chinese society.

The Legendary Life of Lao-tzu

There are many legends but few hard facts about the life of Lao-tzu. The principal historical account of his life is highly doubtful because it was written around four hundred years after his death. Some scholars have even argued that he may be an entirely mythical figure.

One legend about Lao-tzu's birth emphasizes his great wisdom. It tells that Lao-tzu's mother was a virgin who carried him in her womb for no fewer than eighty years, and his father was a beam of sunlight. With such origins and after such a long gestation period, the philosopher, on the day of his birth, was as wise as an eighty-year-old sage and had a full head of gray hair.

In adulthood, Lao-tzu occupied the position of diviner to the royal court of the Zhou dynasty, where he is reputed to have taught Confucius himself. Taoists like to say that Confucius was Lao-tzu's worst pupil; according to the Taoist scholar Zhuangzi (Chuang-tzu), when Confucius sought out Lao-tzu, determined to talk to him about humanity and duty, Lao-tzu reputedly said: "Seagulls do not become white by washing themselves every day; crows do not become black by dipping themselves daily in ink. In these cases, black and white are natural characteristics, so it cannot be said that one is better than the other. One who understands the Tao and employs humanity and duty to distinguish between good and evil is making the same mistake." Confucius was said to have been so impressed by Lao-tzu that he likened his teacher to a dragon riding the wind and clouds of the heavens.

According to other legends, as the Zhou dynasty began to decline, Lao-tzu became increasingly disenchanted with his own life and the general social conditions in China. One day, he decided that he could tolerate it no longer and rode off on a water buffalo to the far west. It is said that, shortly before leaving China, he wrote the *Tao Te Ching* (*Classic of the Way and Its Virtue*) and handed the manuscript to the guardian of the mountain pass through which he was traveling. He then took leave of China forever. Some say that he made his way to India, where he taught a modified version of his theories, which became known as **Buddhism**.

Mixing the Three Doctrines

The philosophical religion of Buddhism was imported into China in the first century CE following Chinese contact with central Asia as a result of the silk trade. The three teachings of Confucianism, Taoism, and Buddhism then coexisted in China for several centuries and became known as the Three Doctrines. Few people adhered strictly to any one of these religions; most people mixed and matched elements of all three schools of thought in their religious practices.

The Chongsheng Monastery in Dali, China, is one of the country's largest Buddhist institutions.

Buddhism, which grew from the teachings of **Siddharta Gautama** (the Buddha; ca. 563–483 BCE), was established in northeastern India by the fourth century BCE and came to China principally in the form of the Mahayana (Greater Vehicle) tradition that emerged in the first century CE. The Mahayana form of Buddhist thought viewed the historical Buddha as an incarnation of a transcendent Buddha and emphasized the importance of compassion. It argued that the supreme goal for a Buddhist was to become a bodhisattva, a person who had reached nirvana or enlightenment but chose to return to earth through reincarnation in order to help others toward the same goal.

In the third century CE, Confucianism underwent a complete reinterpretation based on the *I Ching* (*Classic of Changes*), one of the *Five Classics* of Chinese philosophy, and the *Tao Te Ching* (*Classic of the Way and Its Virtue*), a Taoist work attributed to Lao-tzu. Under the influence of those two books, Confucianism developed into a value system that codified and reflected the individual's desire for self-determination and personal salvation.

The Han, who ruled until 220 CE, rejected legalism in 136 BCE and adopted Confucianism as their underlying philosophy of government. They combined Confucianism with ancient Chinese ideas of the cosmos. Rather than simply exercise power, rulers had to legitimize it by determining the will of heaven. The policy was a new manifestation of the old idea of the mandate of heaven, and indeed, the Han emperors became known as the sons of heaven. Heaven's approval or disapproval of imperial rule could be signaled by natural phenomena, such as storms and earthquakes, which were regarded as portents.

In keeping with the teachings of Confucianism, the emperors of the Han dynasty promoted the ideal of universal equality, and they relied upon merit rather than social status when making bureaucratic appointments. They founded an official school—centered around the *Wu Jing* (*Five Classics*)—for political officials, and they required applicants to pass written tests before assuming administrative posts.

Liu Bang, depicted here by an eighteenth-century CE Chinese artist, was the first emperor of the Han dynasty.

CHAPTER THREE

China's Growing Empire

The reign of the Han dynasty (206 BCE–220 CE) was a period of substantial power and economic success in China. However, in the centuries following the ouster of the Hans, the stability of a centralized Chinese state was less certain.

By the end of the third century BCE, the Qin (Ch'in) dynasty had been fatally weakened by rebellions against excessive taxation. Its final collapse, in 206 BCE, was precipitated by an insubordinate army officer named Liu Bang (Liu Pang). At first just one of many rebel leaders, Liu Bang was popular with the masses, possibly because he shared their peasant origins. He soon became leader of the whole uprising. Having established a firm power base, he declared himself emperor, an act that marked the formal foundation of the Han dynasty. Liu Bang was also known as Gaozu (Kao-tsu).

By 202 BCE, Liu Bang had eliminated virtually all internal opposition to his rule, either by force of arms or by diplomacy. He reduced the tax burden on the peasants, who responded by working more efficiently, thereby reviving the rural economy. Liu Bang maintained China's traditional feudal structure and rewarded his allies and relatives with their own hereditary kingdoms.

The kingdoms did not maintain their independence for long. Subsequent Han rulers retook direct control of virtually all the lands in their domain, thereby establishing the dynasty's reputation for reform. The other major change implemented by the Han emperors was the introduction of Confucianism as an official ideology.

Transitioning to Confucianism

The Qin dynasty had set great store in the legalist teachings of Xunzi (Hsün-tzu; ca. 298–230 BCE), a philosopher who took the view that people were by nature evil and needed strict laws and punishments to regulate their conduct. Xunzi gave the Qin emperors a rationale for minimizing individual freedom and for exercising unlimited control over society.

Confucianism, in contrast, regarded the individual as the most important unit in the hierarchies of family, society, and state. Its founder, Confucius (551–479 BCE), developed his philosophy while advising the rulers of various states. He sought to reestablish social order through personal morality, a code of behavior learned by studying the rules of propriety outlined in the literature of the Shang dynasty (ca. 1766–1050 BCE).

The Han emperors maintained the Qin dynasty's administrative apparatus but modified many of its policies to suit their own ends. When they formally adopted Confucianism in 136 BCE, they espoused the philosophy's principle of encouraging learning, on the basis that educated individuals are of greater use to society than unenlightened people.

The Han rulers made it compulsory for holders of public office to pass examinations. This development ensured that officials earned their positions based on merit rather than family connections, as had previously been the case. The study of Confucianism became an essential requirement for government service, and a university for bureaucrats was set up in the late second century BCE. The emperors reorganized the system of taxation, generally reducing the financial burden on the populace and establishing uniform levies throughout the empire to replace excessively complex local laws and currencies. The Han rulers also encouraged people to maintain grain reserves as a precaution against famine.

Han Dynasty Expansion

Under Emperor Wu Ti (ruled ca. 140–86 BCE), the early Han dynasty reached its peak of expansion. In the west, Chinese forces advanced into the valley of the Jaxartes River (in present-day Kazakhstan), where they fought the Xiongnu (Hsiung-nu), an ancient people about whom little is known, other than that they may have been related to the **Huns**. Wu Ti's general, Zhang Qian (Chang Chien), then consolidated China's position through diplomacy, forming alliances with Samarkand, Bactria, Bokhara, and Ferghana. (The remains of some of the forts and fortifications built to hold back the Huns may still be seen in the Gobi Desert.) China then took the offensive in the north and conquered the Tarim Basin. Wu Ti eventually established imperial control over the southern part of Manchuria and northern Korea. In the south, he conquered the island of Hainan. He established colonies in Annam and Korea and ultimately extended Han authority from Korea to Tonkin in Vietnam, although much of the area, especially south of the Yangtze River, was not completely assimilated.

These campaigns cost more money than the Chinese treasury had at its disposal. In an attempt to make up the shortfall, Wu Ti and his successors increased taxation and reintroduced government monopolies, which had been abolished in the early years of the Han dynasty.

Having overstretched itself in foreign adventures, the Han dynasty rapidly lost much of its authority. Its decline was hastened by a series of rulers who came to the imperial throne in infancy. Their mothers governed on their behalf and undermined the established meritocracy by appointing relatives to key government positions. The regencies created an atmosphere of intrigue and partisanship.

The financial situation deteriorated as provincial landholding families, having refused to pay taxes, were given tax-exempt status. The government still needed funds, so it passed the

This statue of a cavalryman was excavated from the tomb of a Han dynasty general.

burden on to the peasants by increasing their indebtedness. For many farmers, working conditions became intolerable. They divided their landholdings among family, friends, and the highest bidders and looked for other means of support. Some former farmers turned to banditry; others took up arms against imperial rule.

Wang Mang

Wang Mang was the usurper who founded the short-lived **Xin (Hsin) dynasty**. His father's half sister was an empress of the Han dynasty. In 16 BCE, Wang Mang was given a noble title and later appointed to the regency. He outmaneuvered his opponents and had his own daughter enthroned as empress under a fourteen-year-old emperor who died suddenly and mysteriously the same year. Wang Mang was accused of murder by his enemies. He solved the succession problem by selecting from the possible claimants a one-year-old boy who was not officially enthroned but called the Young Prince. Wang Mang then assumed the position of acting emperor.

Having subdued his opponents, Wang Mang announced that heaven was calling for an end to the Han dynasty and that he had the mandate to create a new one. On January 10, 9 CE, Wang Mang ascended the throne and proclaimed the foundation of the Xin dynasty.

Wang Mang maintained the agrarian and monetary policies of the Han dynasty. He supported scholarship and led China successfully in its foreign policy. He was an unscrupulous legal hardliner who had three of his own sons executed for breaking the law, along with a grandson and a nephew.

The Xin dynasty was cut short by a natural catastrophe. Between 2 and 5 CE, and again in 11 CE, the Yellow River changed its course, devastating a large populated area. Famine and epidemics led to mass migration and civil war. One of the rebellious peasant groups, known as the Red Eyebrows because they painted their faces to look like demons, defeated Wang Mang's armies. Other rebellions ensued. On October 4, 23 CE, the rebels broke into the capital. The imperial palace was set on fire. Together with around a thousand of his supporters, Wang Mang made a last-ditch defense of his throne, but he was killed in the ensuing battle. The Xin dynasty thus came to an abrupt end on October 6.

Trading on the Silk Road

The **Silk Road** was the earliest trade link between China and Europe and northern Africa. There is evidence that inhabitants of the Sahara Desert were importing goods overland from eastern Asia as early as 7500 BCE. The route became established as a caravan trail in the second half of the first millennium CE.

In China, the terminus of the Silk Road was in Chang'an (modern Xi'an). From there, the route stretched 5,000 miles (8,000 km) westward along the Great Wall of China, then divided into two parallel passages to the north and south of the Tibetan Plateau. The branches rejoined at Kokand (a city in modern Uzbekistan), then went on across Afghanistan and Mesopotamia to the Mediterranean Sea.

The main Chinese export was the silk that gave the trail its name. The eastbound trade was mainly gold, silver, and wool. Few people made the full journey from one end of the route to the other; most people handled the goods for no more than a few hundred miles.

The Han Dynasty Continues

After the fall of the Xin dynasty, the Han returned to power. However, the problem of infant emperors and incompetent regent-mothers reemerged. The situation created administrative chaos that was in sharp contrast to the discipline and order of the early Han period. The emperors turned to the court eunuchs (castrated men) for support, but the latter demanded increased political power in return for their assistance. Factional struggles led first to intrigue and then to open conflict.

The later Han rulers also faced other problems. During the dynasty's earlier decline, many of the great landowners had achieved local autonomy and established their own private armies. In 184 CE, Taoist (Daoist) societies organized rebellions against imperial rule. The Yellow Turbans (a group named for the color of their headscarves) caused devastation in Shandong (Shantung) until 204 CE.

in 626 CE, China was the largest empire in the world. Its generals occupied parts of Turkestan, Korea, Pamir (part of present-day Tajikistan), and Tibet. After the conclusion of favorable treaties with the peoples of central Asia, China dominated the Tarim Basin. The influence of the Tang dynasty was also evident in Japan, southern Manchuria, and northern Vietnam.

Construction of the Grand Canal, the world's longest manmade waterway, was begun during the reign of Yang Jian.

Foreign trade expanded along the overland caravan routes and across the seas through the port of Guangzhou (Canton). One great emperor followed another, and the country prospered as never before. Commercial success was reflected in a golden age of art and literature. In the early Tang era, the capital, Chang'an, was renowned for its culture and religious toleration. Buddhism reached its peak of popularity.

Although the power of the Tang dynasty began to decline in the eighth century CE, the empire's artistic output remained outstanding and prolific. More than one thousand major poets are known from this period. Literature was made more accessible than ever before by the development of printing, which permitted the large-scale production of texts; previously, written works could be reproduced only by manual transcription. The later Tang emperors published a

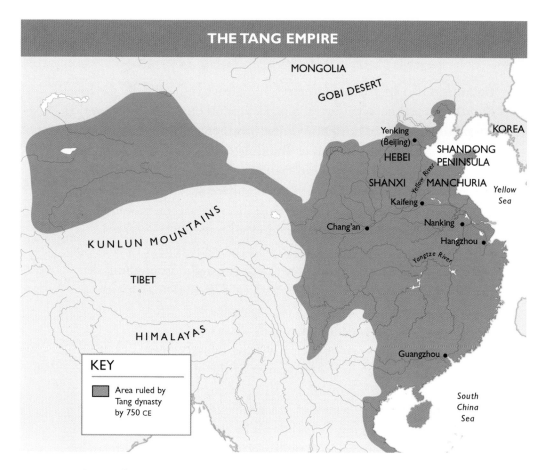

THE TANG EMPIRE

MONGOLIA

GOBI DESERT

KOREA

Yenking
(Beijing)
HEBEI

SHANDONG
PENINSULA

SHANXI MANCHURIA

Yellow River

Yellow
Sea

Kaifeng

Chang'an

Nanking

Hangzhou

KUNLUN MOUNTAINS

Yongtze River

TIBET

HIMALAYAS

Guangzhou

KEY

Area ruled by
Tang dynasty
by 750 CE

South
China
Sea

newsletter for their officials throughout the country. The Tang dynasty also used the new invention to print the world's first paper money.

The peasants' tax liability was calculated on the basis of the amount of land they held. The flaw in the system was that it assessed indebtedness per capita; if a man divided his allotment among two or more heirs, each of them had to pay the same amount as their father had paid even though they had no more than half as much land. The problem was exacerbated by rapid population growth and the resentment caused when some favored people were still granted tax-free status for their estates. Peasants who could not pay the taxes on their allotments ran away, thereby depriving the government of revenue and depleting the army (all adult males were required to perform a period of military service). Eventually, the Chinese were forced to hire foreign mercenaries to serve in the border militia. In 751 CE, the soldiers of fortune were blamed for a defeat by the Arabs that cost the Tang dynasty the Tarim Basin.

Religion During the Tang Dynasty

Buddhism had spread to southern China from India and, by the fourth century CE, had become the religion of around one-half of the world's population. Much of northern China was then converted, and by 600 CE, most of the country was Buddhist. The spread of Buddhism was greatly aided by widespread disillusionment with Confucianism, which had become equated with the maintenance of the status quo and corrupt officials. Buddhism—with its emphasis on morality, detachment from earthly things, and inner tranquility—offered a welcome, untainted alternative. Around the same time, China became increasingly influenced by Taoism (Daoism), a philosophy, founded by the Chinese author Lao-tzu (Laozi; ca. 570–490 BCE), which emphasized harmony with the Way (Tao; Dao) of nature and opposed government interference in individuals' affairs.

The tolerance shown by the early Tang dynasty toward Buddhism and Taoism gave way in the latter part of the era to a revival of Confucianism, particularly among the growing class of public officials. Buddhism came to be regarded as an attack on the social order, something that could not be condoned by the state. While Buddhism was, by this time, too firmly established to be rooted out completely, China's growing fear of the exotic led to the proscription of other foreign cultural traditions. Several Buddhist monasteries were forcibly dissolved, at great profit to the state treasuries.

The Song Dynasty

After the last emperor of the Tang dynasty was deposed in 907 CE, China again experienced a period of internal strife. Five short-lived dynasties followed in sequence in the Yellow River Valley. A number of other kingdoms were established at around the same time, most of them in southern China. In the north, the Khitan Mongol Liao dynasty (907–1125 CE) expanded from Manchuria and Mongolia into parts of China—Hebei (Hopei) and Shanxi (Shan-hsi)—and made Yenking (modern Beijing) the southern capital of a Sino-Khitan empire.

China remained divided until 960 CE, when General **Zhao Kuangyin (Chao K'uang-yin)** seized the throne and declared himself the first emperor of the **Song (Sung) dynasty** (960–1279 CE). By 978 CE,

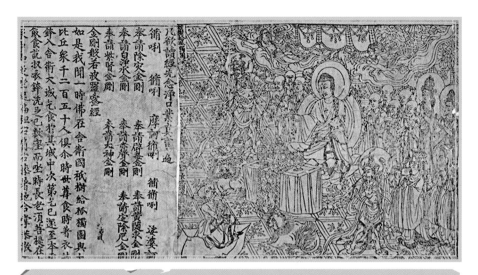

This copy of the *Diamond Sutra*, a Buddhist text, is the oldest dated example of a printed book. It was made in 868 CE, during the reign of the Tang dynasty.

he had reconquered nearly all of China apart from the areas held by the Khitan Mongol Liao dynasty. He made Kaifeng his capital.

The reimposition of order stimulated a revival of trade and general prosperity. Towns expanded, and with their growth came a host of new civic services and amenities: fire departments, municipal police, orphanages, hospitals, public baths, welfare agencies, and even an agricultural testing station. The Song emperors subordinated the army to the civil service and opened the entrance examination for the latter to applicants who were outside the nobility. Education, the arts and literature, philosophy, engineering, astronomy, and mathematics all flourished. Women were allowed to participate in these activities—indeed, a number of the preeminent poets and painters of the age were female.

The military, however, was weakened and suffered frequent defeats by the Liao. In 1004 CE, the Song rulers formally ceded the northern territories that were already occupied by the Liao and agreed to pay them an annual tribute. In 1044 CE, the Song were forced to make further yearly payments to the Xi Xia (Hsi Hsia), a Tangut tribe that lived on China's northwestern border.

Tributes were costly, as were military operations and the maintenance of the large bureaucracy. The economy was unable to keep up with the burgeoning population. There was bitter rivalry over various proposals for reform. To survive, the Song dynasty allied with the Jin (Chin) dynasty (1122–1234 CE) of northern Manchuria against the Liao. Together, they defeated the Liao in 1125 CE. However, the Jin then moved against the Song, seizing Kaifeng in 1126 CE.

The loss of Kaifeng marked the start of the Southern Song era. The Song retreated to Hangzhou and made the city their capital in 1135 CE. As its name suggests, the dynasty controlled only southern China, but its economic and artistic accomplishments outstripped those of the earlier Song dynasty. It showed little sign of any insurmountable problems when it was faced with a new threat, the **Mongols**.

The Mongols Take Over

Around 1200 CE, **Genghis Khan** led the first Mongol horsemen over the Great Wall of China, which marked the southern border of his father's tribal domain. Having inherited the leadership of a loose confederation of nomadic shepherding tribes, Genghis Khan had built an intensely loyal and disciplined fighting force that was characterized by superb horsemanship and archery, extraordinary mobility, and astonishing cruelty.

The Mongols had no desire to forge a lasting empire in China through systematic conquest; their objective was merely seasonal plunder. For years, the Mongol hordes (a horde was a unit of ten thousand soldiers) entered China in the summer to pillage and returned to the Mongolian steppes for the winter. Their marauding power had a devastating effect on morale in China. Many Chinese generals and high officials defected, providing the illiterate Mongols with the services of people who could read and write and who were familiar with technologies previously unknown to them.

In 1213 CE, Ghengis Khan led his armies to the Shandong Peninsula. In 1215 CE, he razed Yenking (modern Beijing), extending his control over the Jin dynasty in northern China. Genghis Khan died in 1227 CE, but his grandsons, Mangu and **Kublai Khan**, eventually completed the conquest that he had started; they seized almost all of China.

Kublai Khan ultimately succeeded to the Mongol leadership in 1260 CE, establishing his capital, Khan-balik (Cambaluc, near modern Beijing), four years later. The city became an international center of great renown. Kublai Khan defeated the Southern Song dynasty in 1279 CE. The rest of China was already in Mongol hands, but the Chinese navy still tried to defend the empire. In the end, the navy suffered overwhelming defeat. The admiral of the fleet drowned, holding in his arms the infant who was the last of the Song emperors.

In the same year, Kublai Khan established the **Yuan (Yüan) dynasty**, becoming its first emperor. Although Kublai Khan was a committed Buddhist and made Buddhism the state religion, he permitted other forms of worship in his realm. He adopted the Chinese bureaucratic system but excluded Chinese people from positions of authority, replacing them with Mongols.

After Kublai Khan's death in 1294 CE, the Mongols chose his grandson as successor. The dynasty remained in power in spite of growing resentment at all levels of Chinese society; the forces of opposition were fatally weakened by conflicting objectives and a lack of common purpose. Chinese officials, primarily Confucians, objected to their reduced status; Chinese peasants, meanwhile, objected to new taxes.

This fourteenth-century CE Persian manuscript shows a mountain battle between Genghis Khan and the Chinese.

Rise of the Ming Dynasty

The first half of the fourteenth century CE saw agricultural shortages and widespread famine, as well as economic inflation and a series of disastrous floods. These crises brought the Chinese people's disaffection to a head, and a number of regional revolts broke out. In the 1360s CE, control of the Yangtze River Valley fell into the hands of Zhu Youanzhang (Chu Yüan-chang). This former Buddhist monk went on to overcome several rival claims to the throne, and in 1368 CE he declared himself Hong-wu (Hung-wu), first emperor of the **Ming dynasty**. The Mings would remain in power for nearly three centuries, until 1644 CE.

Jomon pottery, a product of ancient Japan, is distinguished by its cordlike surface decorations.

CHAPTER FOUR
The History of Japan

Until the end of the Pleistocene epoch, around 10,000 BCE, the three thousand islands that make up present-day Japan were joined to mainland Asia. The earliest vestiges of human occupation—rudimentary tools and piles of mollusk shells discarded after the contents had been eaten—date from around two hundred thousand years ago. The first residents of Japan were hunter-gatherers who arrived from the Korean Peninsula across land that is now covered by the Korea and Tsushima straits and from northeastern Siberia across land that is now covered by the Soya and Tsugaru straits.

Japan solidified into a political entity by no later than the sixth century CE. At around the same time, Buddhism began to spread through the island nation. Over the ensuing thousand years, periods of infighting and civil war alternated with times of political and economic advancement.

Prehistoric Japan

At the end of the Pleistocene epoch, sea levels rose, and Japan took on its modern topographical form—an archipelago off the eastern coast of Asia. By around 7500 BCE, the inhabitants lived mainly by hunting and fishing, although there were still some gatherers who subsisted on nuts and roots. Agriculture developed around this time, as evidenced by the discovery of the remains of blunt axes that appear to have been used for digging soil rather than cutting. The two principal crops were vegetables: yams and taros.

The period's main artistic development was pottery with cordlike surface patterns known as jomon. The word was later adopted as the name for the whole culture. During the next seven thousand years, the decorations became increasingly artistic and ornate, and they developed notable regional variations. Among the other significant archaeological finds from the **Jomon period** are semi-subterranean pit houses with thatched roofs supported by posts.

The Jomon period was succeeded around 250 BCE by the **Yayoi period**. The name is derived from the district of Tokyo in which the earliest artifacts of the period were discovered. Yayoi pottery was less elaborately decorated than Jomon pottery, but it was turned on wheels and fired at higher temperatures than its predecessor, indications that the products were primarily for use rather than for ornamentation.

The Yayoi period also saw the emergence of weaving (whereas Jomon clothing had been made principally of bark) and of metal containers that were used in the cultivation of rice. Rice-growing was new to the area and had probably been imported by refugees from China during the Period of the Warring States (ca. 475–221 BCE).

Birth of the Japanese Empire

The Yayoi period lasted until the second or third century CE, when Japan entered the Iron Age. At some point between that time and 552 CE, the islands became united under an emperor. Exactly how and when that happened is unclear because there are no authoritative contemporary records. The earliest account of Jimmu, Japan's legendary first emperor, appears in *Kojiki* (*Records of Ancient Matters*), an oral-tradition epic that was not written down until 712 CE, at least a century and a half after the events it purports to describe. According to another early (but not necessarily reliable) source, the eighth-century CE *Nihon shoki* (*Chronicles of Japan*), the nation was united by 369 CE, the year in which it dispatched troops to intervene in struggles on the Korean Peninsula.

In Japanese society, the role of the emperor was separated from that of the political power brokers. The ruler's main responsibility was to unite all the religious cults and philosophies that had proliferated regionally before unification. As part of the effort to achieve such unification, the emperor was worshipped as a descendant of the principal deity, **Amaterasu**, the sun goddess (see sidebar, page 53). The emperor was also the head of the *uji* (clans) that practically ruled the country. The uji all had their own gods, but none were as powerful as Amaterasu. The imperial court was situated in the province of **Yamato** on the island of Honshu. That province gave its name to the next period of Japanese history.

Burial Rituals

Much of the knowledge about the history of Japan before the Common Era is derived from archaeological excavations of tombs. The earliest human remains in Japan date from the Jomon period (ca. 7500–250 BCE), during which bodies were buried in small pits, often in the fetal position, with knees tucked under the chin. Some bodies had their hands placed together on their chests and clasped stones, which are thought to have had some mystical significance; most of the pre-Buddhist religions in Japan were fertility cults.

Such burial practices were maintained by the Yayoi people, but by the third century CE, the Japanese had begun to bury their dead in large burial mounds, which were typically circular or keystone-shaped. For that reason, the Yamato period is alternatively known as the Tumulus (Tomb) period. The artifacts discovered in such earthworks demonstrate that, by that time, the Japanese attached great importance to weapons, which were often buried with their owners. Such tombs also contained hollow terra-cotta sculptures known as haniwa.

Shinto

The emergence of Japan as a cohesive state during the Yamato period was aided and to a large extent implemented by the *be* or *tomo*, communities of workers who provided services to the emperor and the uji in times of peace and took up arms for them in times of war. The most important lasting development under the Yamato

Shinto shrines, such as this one in Yasugi, Japan, are known for their distinctive, ritually prescribed architecture.

was the introduction of Buddhism to Japan from Korea. The religion arrived in Japan around 550 CE. It is doubtful that there was any one, identifiable date for Buddhism's arrival; it is more likely that Buddhism was adopted gradually over many years. Buddhist values became ingrained in Japanese life under Crown Prince Shotoku (ruled 593–622 CE), who also introduced the precepts of Confucianism and a constitution in which advancement was based more on merit than on heredity. The establishment of Buddhism also inspired the first written works in the Japanese language. Buddhism soon developed a uniquely Japanese variant, known as **Shinto**, which became the state religion. It retained that official status until the end of World War II in 1945 CE and still has millions of followers in spite of its disestablishment.

After a period of prosperity, the power of the Yamato court went into terminal decline toward the end of the sixth century CE as uji infighting weakened the court's authority. The clan that became dominant was the Soga, under **Iname** (ruled 536–570 CE) and his son Umako (ruled 570–626 CE). The Soga controlled the succession to the imperial throne but did not become emperors themselves; the title remained in a single family to preserve the unbroken line that could traditionally be traced back to Amaterasu. The Soga introduced a meritocratic system of rank in 603 CE and a comprehensive new code of government in 604 CE. The Soga were also keen promoters of Buddhism.

Kotoku's Reforms

The Soga policies did not meet with universal approval, however, and in 645 CE, the Soga were driven into exile by opposition forces with Chinese aid. In 646 CE, the emperor Kotoku became the absolute ruler of Japan. He abolished private ownership of land and abolished the *be*, giving peasants their freedom and making them leaseholders of the state. These innovations—known as the **Taika Reforms**—led, in 702 CE, to the adoption of a state system closely modeled on that of China under the Tang dynasty (618–907 CE) but altered wherever necessary to suit local requirements. Under the new system—known as *ritsuryo*, a combination of the words *ritsu* (criminal code) and *ryo* (administrative and civil code)—the emperor was confirmed as the absolute ruler and high priest. In practice, however, Japan was governed by two authorities: the Dajokan (the council of state) and the Jingikan (the office responsible for divining the will of the gods).

In a further attempt to provide a counterbalance to the traditional Japanese practice of filling high positions with people of noble birth, the new system introduced a civil service examination that made it possible for ordinary people to gain appointment to government posts based on merit. Before long, however, the college that had been set up to train new candidates fell into disuse. The top jobs again became the exclusive property of noble families.

The ritsuryo system recognized two main classes of common people: freemen and slaves. Some freemen were engaged in manufacturing industries (smiths and tanners, for example), but most

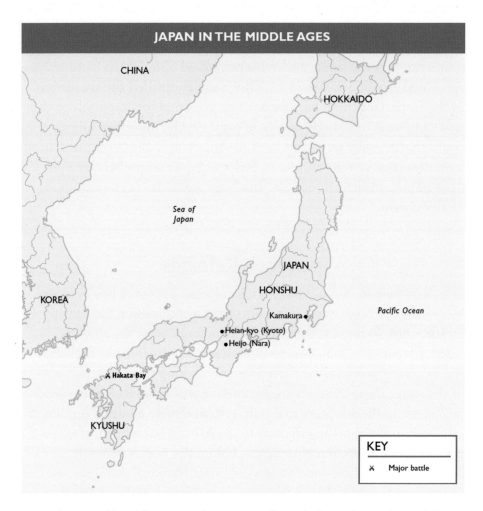

CHINA

HOKKAIDO

Sea of
Japan

JAPAN

HONSHU

KOREA

Kamakura •

Pacific Ocean

• Heian-kyo (Kyoto)

• Heijo (Nara)

✗ Hakata Bay

KYUSHU

KEY
_____
✗   Major battle

were farmers. In addition to their normal work (mainly in the paddy fields), the farmers were required to perform military service and as many as sixty days a year of labor on public works. They also had to bear the cost of transporting their produce to the capital. For freemen in the farthest outlying provinces, this financial burden was too much to bear, and when they defaulted and fled from their land, the central government was powerless to arrest them. In their absence, the state suffered serious losses of revenue.

The slaves belonged to the government, the nobles, and the priests and were supposed to provide their various masters with any service that was demanded. They made up roughly one-tenth of the population.

Before long, it became apparent that Japan was not producing enough food to feed itself. The government responded to the crisis by

The Goddess Amaterasu

Amaterasu—the deity from whom the Japanese royal family claims descent—was born from the left eye of her father, Izanagi, who put her in charge of Takamagahara (the High Celestial Plain), the abode of all the other deities. Amaterasu ruled happily for a time but then withdrew to a cave after arguing with Susanoo, her brother. In her absence, the world was plunged into darkness. The other gods and goddesses eventually lured her out of hiding by telling her that another deity had taken her place.

In modern Japan, Amaterasu is worshipped mainly at the Grand Shrine in the city of Ise, where she is symbolized by a mirror that is one of the imperial treasures.

relaxing its former stipulation that all land was the property of the state and allowing the private ownership of fields used for growing crops. That decision proved to be the death knell of the ritsuryo system.

War with Ezo

In 710 CE, **Heijo** became Japan's first fixed capital; for many years previously, the capital had moved around with the emperor. The design of Heijo was based on the contemporary Chinese capital, Chang'an (modern Xi'an). Heijo did not retain its status for long; in 794 CE, the emperor Kammu (ruled 781–806 CE) transferred the capital to Heian-kyo (present-day Kyoto). In the meantime, the administration's search for new, arable land had taken the Honshu-based government into a war with **Ezo** (the northern part of Japan, roughly coextensive with the island of Hokkaido). For a time, the conflict was so intense that a military draft was introduced; one in three males between the ages of twenty and sixty had to serve in the army for four years.

The Fujiwara Period

From the ninth century to the twelfth century CE, the Japanese aristocracy was headed by the **Fujiwara family**. The Fujiwaras rose to prominence after the Taika Reforms and put an end to interference

This illustration comes from a nineteenth-century CE edition of *The Tale of Genji*.

in affairs of state by the network of provincial temples, monasteries, and nunneries established by the emperor Shomu (ruled 715–756 CE), who had been keen to entrench Buddhist values throughout Japan. The Fujiwara family later married into the imperial family and acted as the emperors' regents. The power of the Fujiwaras peaked in 858 CE, when the head of the family put his own seven-year-old grandson on the imperial throne.

The Fujiwara period witnessed a great flowering of literature. The earliest great work was *Kokin-shu* (905 CE), a collection of more than a thousand poems. At the head of the renaissance were female authors, who tended to write in informal Japanese, rather than the stilted version of Chinese that was then the traditional form in Japan. The two greatest works of the period are *Genji monogatari* (*The Tale of Genji*; ca. 1010 CE), a work by Murasaki Shikibu, a minor noblewoman, and *Makura-no-soshi* (*The Pillow Book*; ca. 1000 CE), a collection of scenes of court life by Sei Shonagon, a lady-in-waiting. *The Tale of Genji* is often described as the world's first novel. It relates the romantic escapades of the courtier of the title.

By the end of the eleventh century CE, much of the land and property that had come into state hands at the time of the Taika Reforms had reverted to private ownership. As a result, the government lost valuable tax revenues and, consequently, much of its power and authority. Go-Sanjo (ruled 1060–1073 CE) was the first emperor in more than a century not to be related to the Fujiwaras. He tried to confiscate large estates without Fujiwara authority and, although his attempt to stop the decline of the state was ultimately a failure, the end of an era was in sight; by 1110 CE, the Fujiwaras had been ousted.

Samurai warriors, like the one seen here in a traditional Japanese silk painting, emerged during the Fujiwara period.

The Samurai and the First Shogun

While the Fujiwaras had lived lavishly and paid little heed to what was going on around them, a new power had emerged in the land—the **samurai**, warriors who gradually took up key positions in provincial government and acquired extensive landholdings of their own. They raised private armies that grew unchecked and eventually became strong enough to challenge the central authorities. When it served their greater purpose, the samurai acted on behalf of the ruling classes. For example, in the eleventh century CE, they helped imperial forces to quell a rebellion in northeastern Japan. Eventually, the Minamoto and the Taira clans (the two leading bands of samurai) confronted each other in the Heiji Disturbance of 1159 CE. The Taira clan won the confrontation easily and became the major power in the land for a generation. However, in 1185 CE the tables were turned, and **Minamoto Yoritomo** set up a new government in the city of Kamakura. In 1192 CE, Yoritomo was named **shogun** (chief military

The Development of the Japanese Language

The Japanese language has no known relatives. Some researchers have tried to link it to the Altaic languages of northern and central Asia, such as Korean, Mongolian, and Manchu. However, those attempts have not been entirely convincing. Japanese has all the hallmarks of aboriginality; it is a language spoken by the inhabitants of a remote island that, until comparatively recently, experienced little outside influence.

Before the modern age, the only foreign country to have any significant effect on Japan was China. Since the earliest times, Japanese has been written with characters borrowed from the script of its mainland neighbor. The oldest written records in Japanese consist of a few names that appear in inscriptions from the late fifth century CE. The earliest substantial Japanese literary texts date from the eighth century CE, although they are known to have been based in part on older texts that have not survived. The language of these works is called Old Japanese.

Phonetic signs were later added to this early script by altering and simplifying a few of the borrowed Chinese characters. Chinese loan words proliferated; even today, more than half the words in Japanese are thought to be of Chinese origin. However, Japanese literary styles and genres have always remained distinct. There are many possible reasons for this, but one of the most important is that Japanese intellectuals often wrote in Chinese as well as in their native tongue, thus maintaining the separate nature of the two languages.

Middle Japanese is the name given to the language that was used in Japan between the late eleventh century and the early seventeenth century CE. During this period, Japanese grammar and vocabulary made their big transition between Old Japanese and the language that is used today.

Old Japanese differs from Middle Japanese and modern Japanese in many ways. Its sound system, for example, had eight different vowels, while the modern language has only five. Old Japanese, however, lacked the contrast between long and short vowels that is so important in the modern language.

commander). It proved to be a pivotal moment in the history of Japan; the country would be ruled by the samurai until the restoration of imperial power in 1868 CE.

The military regime in Kamakura did not replace the civil administration in Kyoto, but the shogunate dominated Japanese affairs and appointed its own vassals. After the death of Yoritomo in 1199 CE, effective power passed to his widow's family, the Hojo clan. Not long afterward, however, a train of events began that would arrest the development of Japan but help establish the Japanese concept of nationhood.

Victory Over the Mongols

In the first fifty years of the thirteenth century CE, the Mongols under Ghengis Khan carved out an empire that extended from the Pacific coast of Asia in the east to Poland in the west. Still seeking new worlds to conquer, the Mongols then turned their attention to Japan. In 1274 CE, an army of Mongols landed in Kyushu and advanced to Chikuzen; at the same time, another Mongol force came ashore in Hakata Bay. The Japanese were ill prepared for such an onslaught, but a typhoon suddenly hit the coast and destroyed most of the invasion force; the survivors withdrew to Korea.

In 1281 CE, the Mongols came again. This time, the Japanese were expecting an invasion and had built defensive walls along their most threatened coasts, but they were still shocked by the size of the force. Again, the attackers brought two armies, one of forty thousand men and another of one hundred thousand men. The Mongols won the first engagement, at Hakata Bay, and it seemed as if their advance would be unstoppable. Just then, however, another typhoon intervened, destroying the invaders' ships at anchor and forcing their armies to break up in disarray. When the storm abated, the Japanese dealt harshly with the Mongols, reportedly killing four-fifths of them. Even then, the Mongols prepared another attack but abandoned the plans when their leader, Kublai Khan (Ghengis Khan's grandson), died in 1294 CE.

The successful defense of their land gave the Japanese a greater sense of common purpose than they had ever had before. They were

This nineteenth-century CE engraving depicts the typhoon that thwarted the Mongol invasion of Japan in 1281 CE.

also convinced that the intervention of the kamikaze (divine wind) on their behalf demonstrated that they were a special race, favored particularly by God.

Renewed Civil War

The Japanese may have succeeded in repelling the Mongol invaders, but the country had ruined itself financially in the process. To make matters worse, the feudal lords were very powerful, and their loyalty to the imperial throne was minimal. When Go-Daigo became emperor in 1318 CE and tried to get rid of the shoguns, he was exiled. He raised an army and regained power in 1333 CE, but he failed to reward adequately his main helper, Takauji of the Ashikaga family. Takauji retaliated by setting up a rival emperor, and for almost sixty years, there were two imperial Japanese courts, one at Kyoto and the other at Nara.

Japan was reunited in 1392 CE; Kyoto was retained as the capital. The early years of the fifteenth century CE saw the rise of a merchant class that grew rich through increased trade with China and Korea.

However, Japan's economic growth suffered a damaging setback when a dispute over the succession to the shogunate led to the Onin War (1467–1477 CE). During and after this civil conflict, the Ashikagas lost all real power, although they remained nominally in control. In the absence of a strong central government, the various lords of Japan—now mainly powerful landowners known as daimyo—vied for supremacy. As a result, the Onin War was merely a precursor to a much longer period of conflict, known as the Sengoku period. This time is also known as the Period of the Warring States, after its earlier Chinese equivalent.

The first Europeans came to Japan during the late Sengoku period, in the 1540s CE. The muskets they brought with them radically altered the nature of warfare in the country. The Europeans also imported Catholicism; Jesuit priest **Francis Xavier** arrived in Japan in 1549 CE and immediately set about his missionary work. Eager to establish trade with Portugal, Japan's rulers encouraged the spread of Christianity, and the two nations soon became close economic partners. Back in the West, explorers described Japan as a convoluted mesh of small, independent fiefdoms (each buying its legitimacy by paying tribute to the emperor) that were slowly coalescing through military and economic partnerships.

The ruins of Harappa, a vestige of the Indus Valley civilization, are located in eastern Pakistan.

As the caste system developed, the divisions between each stratum of society tended to increase. Shudras became isolated; other castes were required to avoid them because contact was said to cause impurity. Shudras were excluded from religious ceremonies; no brahmin was permitted to accept a drink of water from a shudra, although he could accept a gift. There were even rules specifying the correct form of interaction between castes. According to the scripture called the *Atharva Veda*, a brahmin receiving a gift from a shudra must accept it in silence, while he should accept a gift from another brahmin with holy words, a gift from a kshatriya with thanks spoken aloud, and a gift from a vaishya with thanks murmured under his breath.

Civilization on the Ganges

For five centuries, the seminomadic Aryans left little physical trace of their presence, but a mythic record of their migrations and wars with the indigenous peoples has been preserved in the **Vedas**, the holiest books of the Hindu religion, which were transmitted orally

These earthenware horses from the second millennium BCE are an early artifact of the Aryan people.

for centuries until they were written down in the sixth century BCE. Around 1100 BCE, the Aryans adopted ironworking, possibly without outside influence, and soon afterward moved east to settle as rice farmers in villages on the plains of the Ganges River. The appearance on the Gangetic Plain, around 1000–800 BCE, of painted grayware pottery has been linked to Aryan settlement in the area. By 900 BCE, small tribal kingdoms and aristocratic tribal republics, known collectively as *janapadas*, were developing across the Gangetic Plain. By 700 BCE, they had coalesced into sixteen *mahajanapadas* (great realms). By around 500 BCE, Magadha, under King Bimbisara, had emerged as the most powerful janapada. Hand in hand with the process of state formation came the growth of cities, many of which, including Ujjain and Kausambi, had mud-brick defensive walls. Around the same time, there were great developments in religion; it was the formative period of **Hinduism**, and the late sixth century BCE witnessed the lives and teachings of Mahavira, the founder of **Jainism**, and of Siddhartha Gautama, the Buddha himself.

By 500 BCE, the Gangetic civilization extended as far south as the Godavari River. Still farther south, there were iron-using, tribally organized farming peoples, many of whom buried their dead in megalithic cists (box-shaped tombs). Only toward the end of the first millennium BCE did state formation and urban development start in this area.

The Mauryan Empire

In 500 BCE, northern India was divided into several Hindu kingdoms, the most powerful of which was Magadha, ruled by King Bimbisara. Southern India was still dominated by tribal peoples under Hindu influence. In 364 BCE, Magadha came under the control of the expansionist Nanda dynasty, which dominated northern India by around 340 BCE. The dynasty's reputation for oppressive taxation, however, led to their overthrow in a coup d'etat by **Chandragupta Maurya** (ruled ca. 321–293 BCE). Chandragupta's origins are obscure, but he appears to have been a military commander in the northwestern border provinces at the time of Alexander the Great's invasion of the Indus Valley. He fought against Greek outposts in the area and may have met Alexander.

Aryan Learning

The Aryans believed that the universe was built on rita (order) and were inspired by this conviction to investigate natural forms and laws. They made astonishing breakthroughs in mathematics and medicine.

The familiar digits 1, 2, 3, and so on, were first developed in India around 400 BCE. (They are known in English as "Arabic numerals" because they first came into use in Europe via the writings of Arab mathematicians who had learned the use of the numbers from India.) By the start of the Common Era, Indian mathematicians were using advanced concepts such as zero, decimal places, and even algebra. The Aryans also made significant advances in geometry.

Aryans believed that their sacrificial rituals had to be performed exactly as dictated by tradition, using precisely the right words and on altars in a fire pit of the right dimensions. Priestly manuals called *Sulbasutras* (dating from around 800 BCE and attached to the Vedas) gave detailed instructions on the building of the altars and fire pits. The *Sulbasutras* show advanced knowledge of geometry and contain versions of the Pythagorean theorem (the formula, later attributed to the sixth-century BCE Greek mathematician Pythagoras, for calculating the length of the longest side of a right-angled triangle using the lengths of the other two sides) and a number of accurate values for π (the ratio of a circle's circumference to its diameter).

Doctors in India developed the medical system of Ayurveda (life knowledge), which is still in use today. Ayurveda used only herbal and other natural remedies and had eight principal areas: within the body; ear, nose, and throat; mothers, birth, and babies; pediatrics; infertility; toxicology (the study of poisons); mental illness; and surgery. As early as the eighth century BCE, doctors in India could perform cataract surgery and even plastic surgery (for example, to rebuild a damaged nose).

By 311 BCE, Chandragupta had extended his kingdom to the Indus River, an advance that brought him into conflict with Seleucos, who had seized power after Alexander's death. In 305 BCE, Chandragupta defeated Seleucos and was ceded control of the whole Indus Valley in return for five hundred war elephants. Chandragupta maintained a large standing army and imposed a harsh penal code on his people. He also created an effective central bureaucracy, which controlled economic activity and carried out road building, irrigation, and other public works. Around 293 BCE, Chandragupta abdicated in favor of his son, **Bindusara** (ruled ca. 293–268 BCE), and became a Jain monk, dying around 286 BCE. Bindusara maintained his father's expansionist program and extended the **Mauryan Empire** far into southern India. In 268 BCE, he was succeeded by his son **Ashoka** (see sidebar, pages 72–73), one of India's most remarkable rulers. Reportedly overcome with remorse after a bloody conquest of the eastern coastal district of Kalinga in 261 BCE, Ashoka converted to Buddhism around 260 BCE.

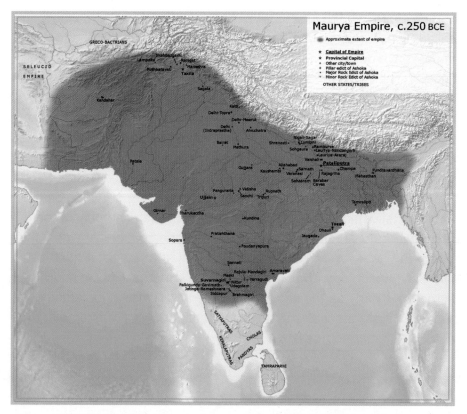

Buddhism had its origins in the teachings of Siddharta Gautama, the Buddha (ca. 563–483 BCE), in the heartland of Magadha. Buddhism began as just one of many sects influenced by, but reacting against, India's traditions of Brahmanic Hinduism. The missionary work started by Ashoka in 258 BCE began its transformation from minor sect to major world religion. Ashoka adopted the Buddhist principles of right conduct and nonviolence, assured neighboring states of his goodwill, ameliorated his grandfather's penal code, and sought to rule as far as possible by moral authority alone. To spread Buddhist values, he had edicts on morality and compassion carved on rock faces and pillars throughout his empire. More than thirty of these inscriptions survive, forming the most important source of information about Ashoka's reign. Ashoka intervened in doctrinal matters, and it was his initiative that led to the defining of the Buddhist canon at the Third Buddhist Council at Pataliputra around 240 BCE. Ashoka also promoted Buddhism abroad, sending missions to Indonesia, southern India, Ceylon, the Greek states of western Asia, and the nomads of central Asia.

Although Ashoka's empire was the largest state to exist in India before the coming of the **Mughals** in the seventeenth century CE, it did not long survive the ruler's death in 233 BCE. Much of Ashoka's empire was held only loosely, and the south was lost almost at once. By 200 BCE, the Bactrian Greeks had conquered the Indus Valley and restored Alexander's frontier in India. In the 180s BCE, the Bactrians briefly extended their control as far south as Barygaza and as far east as Mathura. The last Mauryan king was overthrown in 185 BCE by Pushyamitra Shunga, one of his generals. Under the Shunga dynasty, Magadha remained a major power, but after the dynasty fell in 73 BCE, the kingdom's power collapsed completely, and it became just one minor state among many on the Gangetic Plain. By that time, power had shifted to the northwest, where the Sakas, nomadic invaders from central Asia, had established a powerful kingdom around 94 BCE. By the beginning of the Common Era, the Saka kingdom was in decline, but around the year 50 CE, a second wave of nomads, the Kushans, invaded and founded another major kingdom in the northwest.

The Life of Ashoka

Born around 304 BCE and ruling from 268 to 233 BCE, Ashoka held sway over more of the Indian subcontinent than any ruler before him. After his death, it was not until the height of the Mughal Empire—almost two thousand years later—that anyone controlled as much of India as he had. There is clear evidence of Ashoka's achievements as a ruler on the stone monuments inscribed with his sayings and orders. On one of these monuments is a sculpture of four outward-facing lions, which has become the official symbol of modern India.

Ashoka was born into the Mauryan dynasty that ruled extensive areas in northern India. There are many legends about Ashoka's ancestry and childhood, and most of them are designed to emphasize his link to the Buddha. There are also many stories of Ashoka's youthful rivalry with his older brothers; according to one tale, he came to power by killing them all. Whether that is true or not, there is no doubt that, in the first eight years of his reign, Ashoka extended Mauryan power in

This stone pillar, topped with four lions, is one of India's many reminders of the reign of Ashoka.

a relentless series of campaigns across India, creating an empire that stretched from what is now Bangladesh in the east to what is now Iran in the west, and from the Himalayas in the north to include all but the southern tip of peninsular India. Ashoka's capital was Pataliputra, modern-day Patna in the state of Bihar.

Ashoka conquered the state of Kalinga on the east coast of India, probably around 261 BCE. The conquest was particularly bloody, and historians have estimated that one hundred thousand Kalingans were killed.

Apparently, the brutality of the conquest of Kalinga deeply affected Ashoka, and he adopted Buddhism as a response. One of his early wives, Devi, is said to have been a Buddhist who greatly influenced him.

There is no doubt that Ashoka tried to mold his empire into a coherent state with Buddhist principles at its core. He built numerous stupas (Buddhist shrines)—according to some sources, as many as eighty-four thousand (traditionally, the number of ashes into which the body of the Buddha disintegrated). In line with Buddhist teachings, Ashoka forbade hunting except for food. He encouraged vegetarianism and herbal medicine and created a road system to facilitate pilgrimages to the most important Buddhist sites. He ended his policy of violent conquest, and Mauryan India enjoyed good relations with the Greek world. Ashoka also sent Buddhist missionaries out from India to all the surrounding states. Principles of tolerance for all religious groups were carved for all to see. That may have been common sense in a highly diverse empire, but it was unusual in the ancient world.

According to the Vedic creation story, Purusha, shown here, was the first man and the source of all things.

CHAPTER SIX

The Rise of Hinduism

Hinduism, as we know it today, had more or less solidified in India by the fifth century CE. It grew primarily out of the beliefs and rituals of the Aryans, who, in around 1500 BCE, migrated to the Indus River Valley. Rooted in oral tradition, the Aryan faith was eventually codified and written down in the Vedas, the earliest of which date to about 1200 BCE. This Vedic religion, as it came to be known, subsequently took on a number of external influences—from Jainism and Buddhism, and from a series of invasions by European peoples between 200 BCE and 500 CE. Modern Hinduism is a result of this blending of traditions.

Ancient Indians did not call their faith Hinduism, however. The word was not used until the nineteenth century CE, although it derives from the ancient Indo-European nomads' name for the Indus River. In ancient India, the faith was called Sanatana Dharma (Eternal Law) because it was said to have always existed. The Vedas, the scriptures of the Aryan nomads and their descendants, were classed not as *smriti* (recalled) but as *shruti* (heard); they were presented as the result of firsthand experience. Adherents believed that the faith had no founder because it had existed from the beginning of all things; it represented a statement of the natural law that governed material and spiritual reality and that applied—like the law of gravity—regardless of whether people were aware of it or paid respect to it.

The Vedic Religion of the Aryans

The warlike Aryans worshipped a range of nature deities and practiced a ritualized religion based on sacrifices performed by priests in sacred fire pits. The nomads' religion blended with that of the indigenous peoples of the region, descendants of the Indus Valley people, whose civilization had thrived from around 2600 to 2000 BCE and who, judging from the remains of cities at Mohenjo-Daro and Harappa (in modern Pakistan), worshipped the bull and a horned storm god believed to be a forerunner of Shiva, one of the principal deities of Hinduism.

This seal, found at the ruins of Mohenjo-Daro, suggests that the Indus Valley civilization worshipped bulls.

The Vedic deities were primarily beneficent, and delivered prosperity to their worshippers. When natural disaster or other calamity struck, it was not through divine anger, as in the Judeo-Christian tradition, but through the actions of the gods' powerful enemies, the demons. The principal deities were male gods; goddesses were cast in supporting roles, reflecting the patriarchal organization of Aryan society.

Vishnu had ten **avatars** (incarnations). His first avatar was as
Matsya, half-man and half-fish, who saved Manu (a figure comparable
to Noah in the Judeo-Christian tradition) from a great flood and
destroyed a demon named Hayagriva (Horseneck), who had stolen the
Vedas from Brahma. Matsya retrieved the Vedas and gave them back
to Brahma. The second avatar was as Kurma, the turtle who supported
the mountain with which the gods churned up the cosmic ocean and
brought forth a number of sacred emanations, including the divine drink
(amrita) and the goddess Lakshmi.

Vishnu's third avatar was as the bull Varaha, who killed a demon
named Hiranyaksha (Eye of Gold), rescued the earth from the bed of the
cosmic ocean, and again retrieved the holy Vedas. His fourth avatar was
a lion, Narasimha, who killed another wicked demon, Hiranyakashipu.
In his fifth avatar, Vishnu took the form of a dwarf named Vamana; he
came into being to thwart the wicked plotting of an earthly king named
Bali. Bali had taken possession of the universe, including the abode of
the gods, but Vamana tricked him into giving them back. He persuaded
Bali to agree to give him as much land
as he could encompass in three strides.
Vamana then abandoned the body of
the dwarf and grew enormously so that
his three steps measured out the entire
universe, including the home of the gods.
Bali gave the lands back and was made the
god of the underworld.

In his sixth avatar—as a priest
named Parashurama—Vishnu defeated
a hundred-armed warrior who was
undermining dharma by threatening the
brahmins (priests). In his seventh avatar,
Vishnu was the god Rama, as described in
the *Ramayana*. In his eighth avatar, Vishnu
became the god Krishna, as detailed in the
Mahabharata. Vishnu's ninth avatar was as
the historical Buddha, Prince Gautama,
the founder of Buddhism. Vishnu's tenth
and final avatar lay in the future, as Kalki,

Matsya, half-man and half-fish,
was the first of Vishnu's ten avatars.

who would arrive to end creation either as a warrior on a white horse or as the horse itself.

Vishnu was usually represented with dark-blue skin, riding the golden-bodied man-bird Garuda, who, in the Vedas, brought nectar from heaven to earth. Vishnu had one empty hand (as a giver of gifts), one hand holding a discus (symbolizing the sun) or a wheel (the cycle of births and deaths), another hand holding a conch shell (from which the elements were created), and the fourth hand holding a lotus (symbolizing his creativity).

Rama and Krishna

The exploits of Vishnu's seventh avatar, Rama, were probably based on those of a historical prince from around 1000 to 700 BCE. The story of how Rama rescued his wife, Sita, after she was kidnapped by the demon king of Sri Lanka was told first in the *Mahabharata* before being developed in the later *Ramayana*. By the start of the Common Era, the figure of Rama had been incorporated into the religious tradition of the god Vishnu and established as one of his avatars. Rama became a very popular god in his own right, revered as an exemplar of loyalty and bravery. He was usually depicted with blue skin and wearing a tall cap.

Likewise, the story of Krishna, which told how the god defeated Kamsa, the evil ruler of a northern Indian people named the Yadavas, was a blend of historical fact and religious tradition. The factual elements were derived from the life of a historical hero of the Yadavas and combined with tales of a flute-playing forest god of southern India. Seen as an avatar of Vishnu, Krishna was also a very popular god in his own right. As an infant, Krishna was sent away from the court to be raised in the safety of a forest village. There, he dallied with the *gopis*, the wives of the local cowherd, and in particular with his favorite, Radha. Krishna was often depicted with blue-black skin, wearing a headdress of peacock feathers and playing his flute. During his forest childhood, Krishna killed a five-headed snake demon named Kaliya.

Shiva, the Destroyer

Shiva united many contradictory qualities in a single person. He was creator as well as destroyer, both benign and malevolent. He gave

The Three Ashramas

The older Vedas identified three *ashramas* (goals of life) as follows: *artha* (wealth or material success), *kama* (sensual pleasure), and *dharma* (right social behavior). The Vedas also described the obligations that a person was expected to meet in three stages of life: first, as a *brahmachari* (student); second, as a *grihastha* (householder), when he fulfilled duties to spouse, family, and local community; and third, as *vanaprastha*, a hermit or denizen of the forest who withdrew from material concerns to concentrate on religious matters. The Upanishads described a fourth stage, that of the *sannyasin* (renouncer), who foreswore all obligations and focused on achieving *moksha* (release from the cycle of birth and death).

expression to the anger of the avenger as well as to the benevolence of the restorer. He was celebrated both as an ascetic mystic and as a great lover.

Shiva had five main aspects. The first was as a holy man, seated on Mount Kailasa in the Himalayas, who, by the power of his meditation, generated the *tapas* (energy that sustained the universe). The second aspect was as the four-armed god Nataraja, who danced on top of the dwarf of ignorance while holding the fire of destruction and new life and playing the drum of time and creation. Shiva-Nataraja is often depicted with one right hand raised to indicate "Have no fear" and one left hand pointed at the foot he has lifted out of the circle of fire that surrounds him, which offers his devotees escape from the cycle of birth and death.

This eleventh-century CE statue of Shiva-Nataraja casts him in the traditional pose.

Shiva's third aspect was as a fertility god in the form of the lingam, a stone pillar representing the penis and the creative potentiality of life. The fourth aspect was as Bhairava (defeater of demons) or Buteshvara (god of ghosts). Shiva's fifth aspect was as a medicine god, a holy shepherd of the souls of men and a gatherer of healing herbs. Depicted with a third eye, he saved his devotees from destruction by using his hair to break the fall of the sacred Ganges River when it was released from heaven.

Hindu Goddesses

The worship of a mother goddess had ancient origins in India, dating from at least the third millennium BCE, when people of the Indus Valley civilization made statuettes of wide-hipped women that are thought to have been used in fertility rites. Vedic religion, however, was dominated by gods. Goddesses generally had subordinate roles, although several of them were celebrated in Vedic hymns. Among the most prominent were Sarasvati, Ganges, and Yamuna (three river goddesses), Usha (the dawn goddess), Vac (the goddess of speech and poetry), and Aditi (upholder of the sky and sustainer of existence). In the early centuries of the Common Era, however, goddesses achieved independent prominence as objects of worship.

The goddess Kali is often depicted wearing a necklace of human heads.

The principal goddess—known either as Shakti (from the Sanskrit for "energy") or as Devi (from the Sanskrit *div*, meaning "to shine")—took many forms. All the principal gods were worshipped alongside their goddess consorts: Vishnu was accompanied by Lakshmi; Brahma had Sarasvati; Krishna had Radha; Rama had Sita. All these goddesses were seen as aspects of the one great goddess. According to myth, the supreme female goddess is primarily identified as Parvati, bearer of the creative power of womankind.

A daughter of the mountain Himalaya, Parvati became the consort of Shiva. In this role, she is depicted as a woman of unparalleled beauty, but she has two other, darker avatars: Durga and Kali. The former appears as the spouse of Bhairava (defeater of demons, an avatar of Shiva). According to legend, the gods created her to defeat Mahishasura, the buffalo demon. As Kali, Parvati took on a bloodthirsty nature and enjoyed receiving numerous animal sacrifices. Kali is traditionally depicted as a black-skinned goddess, adorned with a necklace made of skulls.

Epics of Hindu Literature

The two great epic poems of India, the *Mahabharata* and the *Ramayana*, are revered by Hindus as the most sacred scriptures. With two hundred thousand lines, the *Mahabharata* is the world's longest poem, seven times longer than the *Iliad* and the *Odyssey* combined.

According to legend, the Mahabharata was first transcribed by a priest named Vsaya, following the dictation of the elephant god, Ganesh. In truth, it is a virtual encyclopedia of folklore, astronomy, law, geography, theories of government, mathematics, and philosophy assembled by priests and poets between 300 BCE and 400 CE. Its main narrative concerns the war between two sets of cousins, the Pandavas and the Kauravas. It contains the Bhagavad Gita (ca. 200 BCE), a seven-hundred-verse poem that recounts the conversation between the Pandava warrior Arjuna and his charioteer, who reveals himself to be the god Krishna (an incarnation of Vishnu). Krishna instructs Arjuna in the nature of ultimate reality and in how to gain release from samsara (the cycle of birth and death) by acting without self-interest in accordance with one's duty (dharma), by pursuing knowledge, and by demonstrating bhakti (devotion) to a personal god.

The *Ramayana*, a forty-eight-thousand-line poem probably compiled between 200 BCE and 200 CE, tells the story of a prince named Rama who set out to rescue his wife, Sita, after she had been kidnapped from Sri Lanka by a demon king named Ravana. Rama succeeded in his mission with the assistance of the monkey god, Hanuman.

Statues of the Buddha are common throughout southern and eastern Asia.

CHAPTER SEVEN

The Buddha and His Teachings

Buddhism took hold in the fifth century BCE, during the lifetime of Siddharta Gautama, its founder. It subsequently spread throughout Asia, including to India, China, and Thailand. The religion is rooted, in part, in the four Vedas, the Indian holy books that also serve as the basis for Hinduism.

Buddhism is often said to be a way of life rather than a conventional religion. It has had a profound effect on the history of Asia, partly because the beliefs of Buddhists are very influential but also because Buddhist monks and nuns, organized in monasteries, played an important role in many societies during the ancient and medieval periods.

Siddharta Gautama, known as the Buddha (Enlightened One) and founder of the philosophical-religious system of Buddhism, was born around 563 BCE in northern India. His father was chief of the Sakya clan, which led to the Buddha being called Sakyamuni (Sage of the Sakyas). Siddharta and his fellow Sakyas were members of the kshatriya, an Indian caste established by Aryan (Indo-European) invaders in the second millennium BCE. The kshatriyas were warrior aristocrats and rulers; above them in the hierarchy were the brahmins (priests), while below them were the vaishyas (farmers and traders, which made up most of the general population) and the shudras (laborers, craftsmen, and servants).

By the time of Siddharta's birth, most of the Vedas—the holy books of the Aryan peoples—had already been composed. The works included the Upanishads, which proposed that the individual soul was eternally connected to a universal divinity residing at the core of all living beings. A key part of the Aryans' Vedic religion was belief in the centrality of ritual sacrifices performed by brahmin priests. Another important element of the religion as it had developed by the sixth century BCE was the belief in reincarnation—the idea that human souls entered a new body after death and lived life again. Individuals were said to go through a cycle of many births and deaths. According to legend, the Buddha himself declared shortly after his birth: "This is my final existence."

The sixth century BCE was a time of socioeconomic and cultural transition in northern India. The use of iron was increasing, trading cities were being established along the Ganges River, and commerce was being transformed as merchants adopted silver and copper coinage on the Persian model. A religious upheaval was approaching, too. New spiritual teachers and movements emerged to compete with the religion of the brahmin priests, challenging the authority of the Vedas and objecting to the Vedic religion's ritualistic nature, its sacrifices, and its elitism. On the crest of the radical new wave were Siddharta Gautama and Vardhamana—also known as Mahavira (Great Hero; ca. 599–527 BCE)—the founder of Jainism.

The Buddha, Siddharta Gautama

Siddharta Gautama was married at age sixteen to a cousin from a neighboring country. The wedding was arranged to promote a political alliance. Siddharta's wife gave birth to a son, assuring the continuation of the dynasty. Siddharta himself led a very sheltered life within his elite social circle. According to Buddhist tradition, it was not until he was twenty-nine years of age that he first witnessed human suffering. The sight appalled him and inspired him to abandon his privileged life and embark on a search for enlightenment (the realization of eternal truth).

Siddharta studied with two yoga masters and devoted himself to meditation. He tried extreme sensory self-denial, but after six years, he rejected asceticism on the grounds that it had not led to his enlightenment. By that stage, he had already gathered five disciples, but they abandoned him when he gave up asceticism. He now chose a middle path, one of moderation, following a lifestyle that was neither ascetic nor self-indulgent.

He taught the doctrine of *anatman* (no soul), according to which people were made up of impermanent combinations of elements or bundles, known as *skandhas*. The skandhas included the body, the emotions, perception, volition, and consciousness. The idea of an immortal individual personality was seen as a damaging illusion that led to self-centeredness, craving, and suffering. *Abutya* (impermanence) was, the Buddha taught, just as fundamental to human existence as *dukkha* (suffering).

According to the doctrine of *pratityasamutpada* (dependent origin), the makeup of an individual was determined by a chain of causation, each link in the chain arising from the previous one and giving rise to the next one. The first link was ignorance, the cause of human suffering. Ignorance led to the will to live, a prerequisite for the consciousness of the mind and the senses. The mind determined the "name and form," the visible and invisible qualities of the human being. The senses permitted contact with the outside world, and such contact led to perception, then to desire, and then to attachment to existence. From existence came birth, old age, death, and rebirth. In Buddhist teaching, there was a connection between life and life, but not in the Hindu sense of the transmigration of an individual atman because, according to the Buddha, the individual soul was only a transitory aggregate of skandhas.

Pratityasamutpada is related to the Buddha's concept of karma (act or deed) because it acted between one bodily existence and another. A person's karma would determine his or her personal attributes, appearance, intelligence, caste, and even species in rebirth. The Buddha said that there were five destinations: (1) rebirth in hell, (2) coming into existence as a starving spirit, (3) being born as an animal, (4) coming back again as a human, and (5) taking form as a god. Karma was unavoidable, not a matter of divine judgment but the effect of a cause.

The initial conditions of present life were determined by a person's past actions, but his or her actions in the present were not fated or predetermined. He or she could choose freely, modifying behavior and changing karma. It was essential to adopt the four right attitudes: compassion, kindness, sympathetic joy, and equanimity. The Buddha also offered five moral precepts: people should not kill, steal, use hurtful language, indulge in sexual misconduct, or use intoxicants.

Achieving Nirvana

The Buddha taught that the goal in life was to achieve release from karma and liberation from samsara by reaching nirvana (literally, "to blow out"). To the Buddha, nirvana meant a condition in which the fires of desire, hatred, and ignorance had been extinguished and the individual had achieved complete detachment. Nirvana was not annihilation but the attainment of the highest form of consciousness.

The Buddha reputedly refused to answer questions about the nature of the universe or about nirvana, considering it pointless to think about those things. He spoke instead about how nirvana could be reached. He considered it a waste of time to seek the beginning and end of things, explaining: "A religious life does not depend on the question of whether the world is infinite or finite, nor whether or not we exist after death … When the fire goes out, do you ask yourself if it has gone to the north or to the south, to the east or to the west?"

This stone Buddha was found in the ruins of Anuradhapura, Sri Lanka. Buddhism spread to the island in the third century BCE.

Monastic Life

By the fifth century BCE, there was a well-established tradition in India of holy men who traveled the country in good weather and took refuge in forest clearings during the annual monsoon. The Buddha himself is said to have gone on a forest retreat in a secluded spot near Benares (modern Varanasi). In time, the various centers originally built as refuges from the rain became viharas (permanent Buddhist monasteries).

The Buddha taught that, although anyone could attain nirvana by following the Eightfold Path, people freed of worldly cares had a better chance of succeeding. He did not suggest that a monk or a nun was better equipped than a layperson to reach that goal, but he did point out that life in a sangha (monastic order) provided a way to achieve it. Monasteries were open to men and women alike, from any walk of life and from any caste, although escaped slaves, debtors, soldiers, and people in the service of a sovereign were excluded.

Buddhist monks and nuns were subjected to strict discipline, which varied considerably from one tradition to another. No monk or nun was permitted to have sexual relations, steal, kill, or pretend to have supernatural power. Offenses were punishable by expulsion from the order. Joining an order was easy; novitiates shaved their head, put on a habit, and made a declaration in the presence of an older monk or nun. The ordination was a ceremonial occasion that involved extensive questioning and culminated in the assumption of a new name to symbolize a break with the person's old life.

Sanghas depended on the laity because the monks and nuns were unproductive. That tradition had many practical repercussions. Because the greatest benefactor of sanghas was often the sovereign, Buddhism became a part of the political world. Although monks and nuns were allowed to own virtually nothing, the monastic community as a collective could accept generous donations, particularly of land. A sangha could own land worked by lay farmers who gave part of the harvest to the monks. At certain times, monks also engaged in commercial activity. Sanghas were often situated around relic shrines and became pilgrimage centers. Some sanghas aggressively demanded donations and became a burden on the districts in which they were located.

Buddhist Sects

In the centuries following the Buddha's death around 483 BCE, the community of his followers split into a number of sects. Ancient Buddhist texts refer to eighteen schools, but in chronicles, there are references to no fewer than thirty different groups. The Buddhists were still united when they met in a first council of followers at Rajagriha (modern Rajgir) in northeastern India, seeking to agree on what the Buddha had said and to record his words. However, a split occurred at a second council in Vaishali (in the modern state of Bihar) around 383 BCE. A group of monks in the Vajjian

Confederacy had strayed from accepted practice by using money and drinking wine, and although the council censured their activities, the condemnation was not unanimous. The liberal Mahasanghikas (Great Assembly) split from the more traditional Sthaviras (Elders).

The Mahasanghikas had come to an understanding of the nature of the Buddha that was different from that of their fellow Buddhists. Rather than regarding the Buddha as a human who had found enlightenment, they argued that he was an eternal being and that Siddharta Gautama had been created as an apparition of the transcendent Buddha to help people understand him. That concept was important in the later Mahayana form of Buddhism.

The Sthaviras later became known as Theravadins. From their original base in southern India, they spread to Ceylon (Sri Lanka) in the third century BCE. Their form of Buddhism was known as Theravada (Way of the Elders) or Shravakayana (Vehicle of the Disciples) by those who followed or revered it, and as Hinayana (Lesser Vehicle) by those who did not.

Stupas, like this one in Kathmandu, Nepal, are important religious centers for some sects of Buddhism.

enlightenment was achievable by anyone and that the best way to reach it was by suddenly bursting through patterns of habitual thought. Zen had a great influence on the culture of Japan.

When these Tibetan monks finish creating their sand mandala, they will destroy it. This practice reflects the Buddhist doctrine of *abutya* (impermanence).

In the seventh century CE, another school of Buddhism developed in northern India from a blend of the Mahayana tradition and folkloric beliefs. Known as the Vajrayana (Diamond Vehicle) or Tantric Buddhism, it taught the use in religious life of esoteric mystical-magical texts called tantras and secret rituals called mudras. Vajrayana arose around the same time as a similar tantric movement in Hinduism. Vajrayana is characterized by the use of mandalas (maps that symbolize spiritual reality) and the mantra (a sacred syllable chanted as a focus for meditation). Vajrayana was introduced in Tibet in 747 CE by the Indian monk Padmasambhava, and it became the predominant religion in that country. Around the fifteenth century CE, Tibetan monks began to regard the lamas (abbots) of their monasteries as reincarnations of bodhisattvas and the principal one, the Dalai Lama, as the ruler of the country. The theocracy was ended when China seized Tibet in 1951 CE.

Amidism (Pure Land Doctrine) was another school of Mahayana Buddhism to emerge. It began in India but first came to prominence in China around the fourth century CE and was carried to Japan around the ninth century CE. It emphasized belief in a transcendent, compassionate Buddha known in Japanese as Amida. Followers were taught that merely by believing in Amida, by hearing or repeating his name, they could be reborn in his western paradise, the Pure Land.

As Buddhism took root throughout Asia, it was simultaneously waning in the country of its birth. Hinduism, which had more or less solidified by the fifth century CE, began to attract wider interest in India, at Buddhism's expense. A more decisive blow to the religion came in the twelfth century CE, which saw the Turkish conquest of northern India and the subsequent spread of Islam to the region. Buddhism enjoyed a new wave of popularity in the twentieth century CE, however, when the politician and scholar Bhimrao Ramji Ambedkar (1891–1956 CE), born into the lowest rung of Indian society, converted about 3.5 million of his fellow untouchables to the teachings of the Buddha.

The twenty-eight cave monuments at Ajanta, carved into the side of a cliff, were begun during the reign of the Gupta Empire.

CHAPTER EIGHT

India's History Continues

I ndia's history during the Middle Ages is marked by much political upheaval and territorial conflict, with one dynasty after another gaining and losing power. The period also saw the continued spread of Hinduism, Buddhism, and a newcomer to the region, Islam.

In the fourth century CE, the **Gupta Empire** emerged in northern, central, and western India. The earlier Mauryan dynasty, which was at its height under the Buddhist ruler Ashoka (ca. 268–233 BCE), had collapsed in the second century BCE, and five hundred years of political instability followed. The Guptas came to power at a time when the Kushan dynasty, which was of central-Asian origin, was losing power in the north and northwest of India.

The Gupta dynasty was Indian in origin and probably came from Bengal. It rose to power in the fourth century CE under Chandragupta I, a chieftain from Magadha (part of modern Bihar), who gained control of lands farther north by marriage. He subsequently extended his territory west as far as Kausambi (modern Allahabad). Chandragupta I took the title *maharajadhiraja* (king of kings) around 320 CE. His son, Samudra Gupta, was a great conqueror who, between 335 and 375 CE, built on his father's solid foundations. The Guptas won control of the major portion of northern India, while Assam, Nepal, Punjab, and enormous parts of the south paid tribute to them. Samudra Gupta's achievements were recorded in an inscription on one of the pillars originally raised by Ashoka at Kausambi. Samudra Gupta called himself

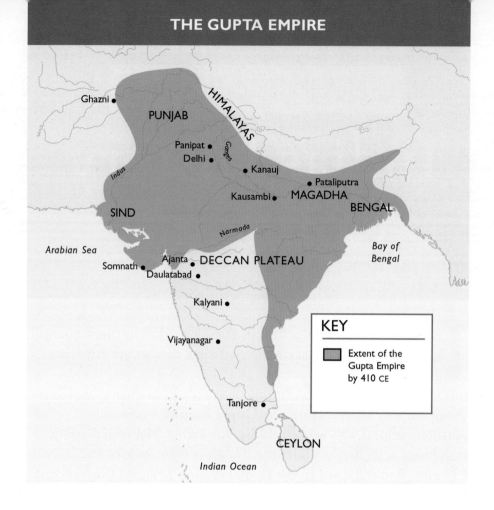

Ghazni

PUNJAB

HIMALAYAS

Panipat
Delhi

Ganges

Kanauj

Indus

Pataliputra

Kausambi   MAGADHA

SIND

BENGAL

Narmada

Arabian Sea

Bay of
Bengal

Somnath   Ajanta   DECCAN PLATEAU
Daulatabad

Kalyani

Vijayanagar

KEY

Extent of the
Gupta Empire
by 410 CE

Tanjore

CEYLON

Indian Ocean

chakravartin (king of the world). After defeating nine kings in northern India and twelve kings in southern India, he performed a prestigious *ashwamedha yajna* (horse sacrifice) to celebrate his success.

The Gupta Empire reached its peak under Samudra Gupta's son, Chandragupta II (ruled 375–414 CE). At the height of its power, the empire extended from the northern border of modern Pakistan to the mouth of the Narmada River and from the mouth of the Indus River to the mouth of the Ganges River. The capital was Pataliputra (modern Patna). Chandragupta II called himself *vikramaditya* (sun of valor).

A Golden Age

The period of Gupta rule, which lasted until the sixth century CE, was a golden age in northern India. The arts and architecture flourished, and the religion derived from the Vedas and the ritual sacrifices of the brahmins began to develop into classical Hinduism. Under the Guptas, who particularly revered the sustaining god Vishnu and called themselves *paramabhagavata* (the principal worshippers of Vishnu), the first great stone temples were erected in northern India. Also around this time, the mother goddess became a popular object of worship, notably in the form of Durga, her incarnation as a consort of Shiva.

Among other developments under the Guptas, the traditional Hindu practice of performing acts of worship in front of an image of a chosen god or goddess became established, while temple design began to take new forms that remained fashionable for centuries. The classic temple structure of the period was a great tower (representing the home of the gods in Mount Meru) set in a courtyard with a central shrine that housed the image of the deity. Within the temples, artists painted splendid murals, and sculptors carved great sculptures. Most of the twenty-eight rock-cut cave monuments at Ajanta in the state of Maharashtra were made during the Gupta era.

The Guptas oversaw a great flowering of literature in Sanskrit. The leading author of the age was the poet **Kalidasa** (see sidebar, page 111). Building on the foundations laid by the sages of ancient India, scientists made many great breakthroughs in mathematics and astronomy. The most famous scientist of the period, Aryabhata (ca. 476–550 CE), developed the use of algebra and made significant advances in trigonometry (the study of triangles). He also calculated the length of the solar year, with extraordinary accuracy, to 365.3586 days and determined that Earth was not stationary but spinning on its axis.

The White Huns

In the second half of the fifth century CE, hordes of warlike central Asian nomads began incursions into India from the northwest, just as the Aryans had done more than a thousand years previously. Little is known of the new invaders, who were called the White Huns, or Hepthalites.

King Skanda Gupta drove back an attempted invasion in 455 CE, but the White Huns continued raiding what is now Pakistan and northwestern India. Their attacks contributed to the collapse of the Gupta Empire, which fragmented into many small states. The White

Huns then took advantage of the lack of central control to mount deeper incursions. Under their leaders, Toramana and Mihirakula, the White Huns made their capital at Sakala (modern Sialkot, Pakistan). Chronicle accounts identify Mihirakula as a self-proclaimed worshipper of Shiva and a violent enemy of Buddhism; he reputedly destroyed many Buddhist monasteries and temples. After the end of the sixth century CE, the White Huns seem to have disappeared. It is possible that they were driven out of India, but it is more likely that they were assimilated into the local population, as other invaders had been before them.

Regional Kingdoms

No empire arose to succeed the Guptas in northern India until the Muslim **Delhi Sultanate** was established in 1206 CE. For more than six hundred years, regional kingdoms and republics rose and fell. In the early seventh century CE, King Harsha of Kanauj briefly reunited parts of the Gupta realm from his kingdom north of Delhi, but his empire was short-lived, barely surviving his death.

Meanwhile, in the region of Bengal, the Pala dynasty rose to power around 750 CE and ruled until 1174 CE. Adherents of Mahayana and Tantric Buddhism, the Pala were responsible for the introduction of Buddhism in Tibet. In northwestern India, the Rajputs (interrelated clans of fearsome warriors ruled by a military aristocracy) established powerful kingdoms in the ninth, tenth, and eleventh centuries CE.

South-Indian Kingdoms

In India, the north-south divide is generally taken to be the Vindhya Range, a broken series of hills, around 675 miles (1,086 km) long, which bisects the country. To the south of the range lies the Deccan Plateau; to the north of the range are the vast northern plains of the Ganges and Indus rivers. Southern India was briefly united in the third century BCE under the Mauryan rulers, but its two principal regions developed separately after the death of the last Mauryan emperor, Ashoka, in 233 BCE.

The Satavahana kings ruled in southern India from the middle of the third century BCE, first as feudatories of the Mauryan Empire

Kalidasa, the Great Writer

The poet and dramatist Kalidasa is revered as the greatest writer in Sanskrit. There is some controversy over when he lived, but many historians place his life in the reign of the great Gupta king Chandragupta II (ruled 375–414 CE). Kalidasa's masterpiece is the play *Abhijnanasakuntala* (*Recognition of Sakuntala*), which treats the mythological narrative of the seduction of the nymph Sankantula by King Dushyanta, founder of the Paurav dynasty. The work is celebrated for its lyricism in describing the beauty of nature and the agony of love lost. Kalidasa also wrote two other plays; two epic poems, *Kumarasambhava* (*Birth of the God of War*) and *Raghuvamsa* (*The Dynasty of Raghu*); and a lyric poem, *Meghaduta* (*Messenger of the Clouds*). Kalidasa was probably a priest in the service of Shiva because his name means "Kali's servant" and the goddess Kali was one of the many forms taken by Shiva's consort, Parvati. The poem *Kumarasambhava* describes the love between Shiva and Parvati and the birth of their son, Kumara, the war god.

but later independently. They were succeeded by the Pallava dynasty, which also began as subordinate (to the Satavahana kings) but rose to independent power in the fourth century CE with a capital at Kanchi (modern Kanchipuram, in Tamil Nadu).

Among the most notable Pallava kings were Mahendravarman I (ruled 600–630 CE) and his successor, Narasimhavarman I (ruled 630–668 CE). Both kings were great patrons of the arts, especially of rock-cut temples. The beautiful monuments at Mahabalipuram (also known as Mamallapuram) were begun during the reigns of these two kings. The works there include temples, carved reliefs, and a monumental structure named the Five Chariots, in honor of Arjuna, Bhima, Yudhishtra, Nakula, and Sahadeva, the leading Pandava brothers in the epic poem the *Mahabharata*. On December 26, 2004 CE, the catastrophic tsunami (tidal wave) unleashed by an earthquake under the bed of the Indian Ocean uncovered parts of what appear to be an ancient city and temple near Mahabalipuram. As the waters receded with enormous force, they pulled back sand that had covered the buildings for centuries. Underwater excavations by the Archaeological Survey of India were stepped up. Local legends support the theory that these may be part of a large Pallava coastal settlement. According to one story, there was once a large city so beautiful that the gods grew jealous and sent a great flood to conceal its glory.

The Pallavas ruled until the end of the ninth century CE, when their former vassals—the Tamil dynasty of the Cholas—destroyed their

The Brihadishvara Temple is a notable example of Chola dynasty architecture.

power base. The Cholas, in turn, founded an empire that comprised all of southern India and Ceylon (Sri Lanka). At times, their armies advanced as far north as the Ganges River. In the early eleventh century CE, the Chola navy under King Rajendra I was the largest ever to sail the Indian Ocean; Rajendra even sponsored a great expedition to the Indonesian archipelago and into Malaysia.

The Chola kings were also great patrons of the arts. Under their rule, superb bronze sculptures were made and large "temple cities" were erected in which the central shrine was surrounded by a multitude of subsidiary shrines, as well as administrative buildings and housing, places for ritual bathing, and even shopping areas. One magnificent example of Chola-period architecture is the Brihadishvara Temple at Tanjore (Thanjavur) in Tamil Nadu. The temple was built between 1003 and 1010 CE by Rajaraja I, founder of the Chola dynasty, in honor of the god Shiva. Its main sanctuary, which contains a simple Shiva lingam (phallic post), stands beneath a tower that is 220 feet (67 m) tall and within a courtyard measuring 500 feet by 250 feet (152 m by 76 m). The complex is known to have employed more than four hundred dancing girls, hundreds of priests, and no fewer than fifty musicians, as well as gardeners, flower gatherers, makers of garlands, cooks, sculptors, painters, and poets.

The Chola were eventually toppled in the thirteenth century CE by another Tamil dynasty, the Pandyas. Under Jatavarman Sundara

Vedanta Philosophy

Vedanta (meaning "end of the Vedas") was a school of Hindu philosophy that was rooted in statements contained in the Upanishads. Vedanta took several different paths and was formalized in the era of the Guptas and afterward in early medieval India. The great mystic and thinker Shankara, who probably lived in the eighth century CE, was the foremost exponent of the branch known as Advaita Vedanta. Advaita Vedanta proposed that all things were ultimately one, that the atman (individual soul) was an aspect of brahman (the divine absolute), and that the apparent multiplicity of the universe was, although real, underpinned on a deeper level by unity; it was finally an illusion (maya in Sanskrit). The soul was initially prevented by avidya (ignorance) from seeing through maya and grasping its identity with brahman, but through the teachings of the Vedanta, it could do so and thus escape the cycle of birth and death. Other Vedanta teachers included Madhva, who lived in the thirteenth century CE and taught that the individual soul existed independently of the supreme brahman, and Vallabha, who lived in the fifteenth century CE and placed great emphasis on the grace of a personal god.

Pandyan (ruled 1251–1268 CE), the Pandya realm expanded as far north as the Krishna River and as far south as Ceylon. However, the power of the Pandyas was ultimately insufficient to withstand the southward expansion of Arab armies in India, and their rule was eclipsed in the fourteenth century CE by the forces of Islam.

The Chalukya Dynasty

On the Deccan Plateau, the kings of the Chalukya dynasty established themselves in the seventh century CE. The dynasty was founded by Pulakesin I (ruled 543–566 CE), who created a great kingdom in the western Deccan Plateau. His capital was at Badami (in the modern state of Karnataka). The dynasty's foremost ruler was Pulakesin II (ruled 610–642 CE), who expanded the borders of the empire in all directions to take in most of the plateau.

After Pulakesin II died, an eastern branch of the family under his brother, Kubja Vishnuvardhana, set up an independent kingdom that

Spreading the Indian Religions

For centuries, the emissaries of Indian princes traveled all over the known world to establish new relationships and to spread the doctrines of their religions. The emissaries sailed to Java, Sumatra, Bali, and Borneo, for example, spreading both Hinduism and Buddhism. The Buddhist temple complex of Borobudur, established in the ninth century CE on the island of Java, is impressive testimony to their evangelical efforts; on the island of Bali in Indonesia, the chief religion is a form of the old Vedic religion with traces of ancient Hinduism. The emissaries also traveled to Cambodia, Burma (Myanmar), and China. In the city of Tamralipti, at the mouth of the Ganges River, ships took on monks as well as cargo. Chinese scholar and pilgrim Yijing (I-tsing), who journeyed to India by way of the Silk Road in 671–695 CE, wrote: "More than a thousand Buddhist monks have applied themselves in the service of scholarship and good works. They investigate and discuss all matters, as they do in India."

ruled from Vengi until the eleventh century CE. Pulakesin II's own branch of the dynasty, the Badami Chalukyas, was eclipsed by the rival Rasthrakuta dynasty, but Chalukya power was restored by the Western Chalyukas, who ruled from Kalyani (modern Basavakalyan in Karnataka) from the tenth century to the twelfth century CE.

The Arrival of Islam

The first contact between Islam and India came in the seventh century CE, through Arab traders whose ships landed on the west coast of the country. Relations between visitors and locals were peaceful at first, with some Arabs marrying into local Rajput families. However, in 711 CE, the plundering of Arab ships by Indian pirates led the Umayyad governor of Iraq to launch an attack under Muhammad ibn Qasim. Arab troops conquered Sind, a region of modern Pakistan, and the conquered people converted to Islam.

Three centuries then passed without further Islamic incursions into India. Then, the Afghan ruler Mahmud of Ghazni launched a series of raids in the eleventh century CE. Descended from Turkish and central Asian nomads who had been driven into Persia and Afghanistan by the western expansion of China, Mahmud made at least seventeen annual expeditions into India from his capital at Ghazni in eastern Afghanistan.

On one of these raids, in 1024 CE, Mahmud of Ghazni led his troops to the great Hindu temple of Shiva at Somnath, near Veraval in western Gujarat. A large gilded lingam was worshipped there. According to an Arab source from the thirteenth century CE, the lingam was washed daily with water from the Ganges River. More than a thousand water carriers brought the water every day, and the temple employed one thousand priests and six hundred musicians, dancers, and servants. Mahmud attacked and looted the temple, personally smashing the lingam with a hammer. More than fifty thousand Indians died trying to defend the temple. According to tradition, the temple destroyed by Mahmud was the third such structure on the site. Little is known of the first temple, but the second was destroyed by Junayad, the Arab ruler of Sind, in 725 CE and then rebuilt. After the attack of

1024 CE, the Somnath temple was destroyed by Muslims on three further occasions—in 1297 CE, 1394 CE, and 1706 CE—and rebuilt each time. The latest reconstruction was completed in 1995 CE.

Mahmud did not establish a lasting presence in India. Although his territory nominally extended from Persia to the Ganges River, in practice, his power in India was restricted to the northern frontier regions, and even there, it was effective only during his annual expeditions.

The Qutb Minar was built to celebrate the Muslim conquests in India.

A Muslim Empire

The first Muslim empire in India was the Delhi Sultanate, which was made possible by the capture of Delhi in 1192 CE by another Afghan ruler, Muhammad of Ghur. The sultanate was ruled by a succession of Turko-Afghan dynasties (see sidebar, page 118), beginning in 1206 CE, when Muhammad of Ghur was assassinated and his general Qutb-ud-Din Aybak took power, proclaiming himself the sultan of Delhi. Qutb-ud-Din Aybak built the Qutb Minar—a brick tower 240 feet (73 m) tall—as a symbol of Muslim victory in India and established the dynasty of the Mamluks. The Mamluk (Slave) dynasty, which lasted until 1290 CE, derived its name from the fact that many of the rulers were slaves or children of slaves who had converted to Islam and won glory as soldiers, thereby raising their social status.

Most subjects of the Delhi sultans were Hindus who were unwilling to accept Muslim rule. Time and again, the Islamic rulers faced uprisings. Only in regions where the Muslims had garrisons and fortifications was there any measure of stability. The Delhi

Sultanate reached its greatest extent around 1330 CE. At that point, Sultan **Muhammad ibn Tughluq** (ruled 1325–1351 CE) attempted to move the capital from Delhi to Daulatabad, a city on the Deccan Plateau from which Muhammad thought he would be able to exert more effective control over the southern provinces. However, his attempts to forge a unified empire failed as provincial governors and nobles rebelled and set up their own independent sultanates, such as the Shahi dynasty in Bengal, which declared independence from Delhi in 1338 CE.

The power of the Tughluq dynasty was severely and lastingly damaged in 1398 CE, when **Tamerlane (Timur the Lame)**, the Mongol ruler of Samarkand, launched a devastating raid on Delhi. In the wake of the Mongol attack, the Tughluq sultans controlled little more than the city of Delhi and its immediate vicinity. Although the sultanate later recovered some of its former territories, the rulers generally resigned themselves to the fact that their rule in India was now no more than nominal.

The Delhi Sultanate came to an end in April of 1526 CE, when Ibrahim Lodhi, the third ruler of the Lodhi dynasty, was defeated near Panipat, north

Babur, seen here in a sixteenth-century CE manuscript, founded the Mughal dynasty.

of Delhi, by the Afghan ruler Babur, a descendant of Tamerlane and Genghis Khan. Babur conquered large areas of India and founded the Mughal dynasty that would rule much of India until the middle of the eighteenth century CE.

The Delhi Sultanate Dynasties

The Delhi Sultanate lasted from 1206 to 1526 CE, when it was eclipsed by the rise of the Mughal dynasty. A succession of Turkish and Afghan families ruled from Delhi during those 320 years.

The first dynasty was that of the Mamluks, established by Qutb-ud-Din Aybak, a Turkish ex-slave who had been the general of Afghan ruler Muhammad of Ghur. The Mamluks ruled until 1290 CE, when they were replaced by another Afghan dynasty—that of the Khalji—founded by Jalal-ud-Din Firuz. Jalal's son, Ala-ud-Din Khalji, repelled a number of attempted Mongol invasions.

The Khalji dynasty was succeeded by the Turkish Tughluq family, which ruled until 1413 CE. The Tughluq dynasty was founded by Ghazi Malik, who ruled as Ghiyath-al-Din Tughluq. The Sayyid dynasty (ruled 1414–1451 CE) rose to power during the period of lawlessness that followed the decline of Tughluq authority after the sack of Delhi by Tamerlane (Timur the Lame) in 1398 CE. The Sayyid dynasty was founded by Khizr Khan.

The rule of the final dynasty of the Delhi Sultanate, the Afghan Lodhi dynasty, began when a military governor in Punjab named Bahlul Khan Lodhi seized the throne in Delhi in 1451 CE. He and his descendants ruled for seventy-five years but lost power when they were defeated at the Battle of Panipat in 1526 CE by the Afghan ruler Babur, who founded the Mughal Empire.

The Bahmani Sultanate

On the Deccan Plateau, the Bahmani Sultanate was established in 1347 CE, when the Turkish governor Ala-ud-Din Bahman Shah rebelled against the Tughluq sultan in Delhi, Muhammad ibn Tughluq. Ala-ud-Din Bahman Shah established a capital at Ahsanabad (modern Gulbarga, in the state of Karnataka). Farther south, the Hindu kingdom of Vijayanagar was established in 1336 CE by Harihara Raya I and his brother, Bukka Raya I. At its height, their empire comprised all of India to the south of the Krishna River. Their capital, Vijayanagar (City of Victory; modern Hampi in Karnataka), was a vast and hugely wealthy metropolis containing arcade bazaars and stone-cut waterways, with beautiful gardens, a great royal palace, and numerous temples. Vijayanagar won fame around the world on the basis of reports from traders and travelers; in 1522 CE, a Portuguese adventurer named Paes reported that it was "as large as Rome" and "the best-provided of the world's cities." Today, the ruins of Vijayanagar cover an area of 15 square miles (40 sq km).

Around 1400 CE, the Bahmani Sultanate divided into five states: Bijapur, Golconda, Ahmadnagar, Bidar, and Berar. The five states waged separate wars with Vijayanagar until 1564 CE, when they allied to win a decisive victory over the Hindu kingdom. The City of Victory was abandoned forever. However, although the kingdoms of the Deccan Plateau were successful in their war in the south, they were exhausted by the struggle, and their resources were depleted. Their weakness paved the way for their defeat and absorption into the Mughal Empire (including Golconda in 1687 CE).

This period had a strong influence on Indian society and culture. Some of the sultanate rulers adopted a moderate level of tolerance toward Islam's rival religions, and, at least to a certain degree, Hindus and Muslims interacted with each other. Meanwhile, Sanskrit lost its status as India's official language; in its place, a number of regional languages gained localized acceptance.

Built on the island of Java in the ninth century CE, the Borobudur temple complex is a marker of the spread of Buddhism throughout Southeast Asia.

CHAPTER NINE
Cultures of Southeast Asia

Although they share common prehistoric roots, the people of Southeast Asia had diverged into a number of different cultures by the end of the first millennium of the Common Era. Between the thirteenth and fifteenth centuries CE, several trading empires thrived in the region.

The earliest known human inhabitants of Southeast Asia lived around forty thousand years ago. At that time, the whole region was one extensive landmass; the seas that now separate the Indochina Peninsula (Cambodia, Laos, Myanmar, Thailand, and Vietnam) from Island Southeast Asia (Indonesia and the Philippines) appeared when global water levels rose by around 150 feet (50 m) between 7000 and 6000 BCE. The comparatively young topography of the region helps explain why many areas of Southeast Asia have more in common culturally and traditionally than their apparent modern isolation might suggest.

A good illustration of the continuity of early civilization across the region may be seen in the archaeological remnants of the Hoabinhian Age (ca. 13,000–4000 BCE). First identified in Vietnam, stone tools of similar design were later excavated in Cambodia, Laos, Myanmar, Sumatra, and Thailand. Some researchers believe that Hoabinhian influence extended as far as southern China, Nepal, Taiwan, and even Australia.

By around 3000 BCE, the rise in sea level had inspired generations of mariners, who traded, settled, and spread their languages across

half the world south of the equator. Southeast Asia's earliest sailors ventured out from Taiwan to Indonesia, Java, the Philippines, and various islands of the Pacific and Indian oceans, where their Proto-Austronesian tongues developed into modern Malayo-Polynesian languages. Today, languages of this group are spoken across the region from Madagascar in the west, through New Zealand and Polynesia, to Hawaii in the east.

Southeast Asia had two other main language groups. One was Tibeto-Burman, which was spoken by Himalayan mountain peoples who moved to lower ground in the eighth century BCE and settled along the Irrawaddy River. Tibeto-Burman developed into Burmese, the language of modern Myanmar. The other language group was Austroasiatic, from which developed modern **Khmer**, Lao, Thai, and Vietnamese.

The Dong Son Civilization

The gradual disconnection of the Indochina Peninsula from developments in Island Southeast Asia is reflected in the increasingly separate evolution of agriculture and metallurgy. By around 2000 BCE, the inhabitants of northeastern Thailand and northern Vietnam were employing methods of cultivating rice and making bronze that were quite unlike those used in the islands and even in neighboring China and India. During the next thousand years, increasingly

The ancient Dong Son civilization is known today for its large bronze drums.

sophisticated metalworking techniques emerged in the Indochina Peninsula. The artifacts discovered at a settlement in northern Vietnam show how far metallurgy had advanced by around 1000 BCE. The village in question, **Dong Son**, has given its name to the whole civilization of the period. The earliest artifacts found there are plowshares, axes, sickles, spearheads, fishhooks, and various items of jewelry. By around 500 BCE, the Dong Son were producing bronze drums that weighed more than 150 pounds (68 kg) and were decorated with geometric shapes and depictions of animals and humans. The similarities between their great stone monuments and those found in the distant islands of Polynesia suggest that the Dong Son were seafarers.

The Dong Son cultivated rice, which had already become the staple diet of the greater part of Southeast Asia. The crop was grown mainly in the fertile plains of the main rivers—notably the Irrawaddy, the Mekong, and the Red—and it was there that the greatest concentrations of population emerged. The upland and mountain areas became—and remain—sparsely populated.

The other main crop was the sago palm, which formed the basis of the diet for people living in eastern Indonesia. The people of Southeast Asia as a whole did not traditionally raise herds of animals, such as cattle or pigs. Much of their protein came from fish, which were farmed in rice fields and ponds. People living near lakes and rivers developed bamboo traps to catch fish, and fishing was the foremost occupation along the coasts.

External Influences

Shortly before the beginning of the Common Era, Southeast Asia came under the influence of its neighbors, India to the west and China to the north. In the late second century BCE, Chinese peoples subjugated northern Vietnam. The conquered region, Annam, remained a distant outpost of the Chinese Empire for more than a thousand years, despite constant opposition from the Vietnamese. The Chinese introduced their own government and their Confucian, Taoist, and Buddhist religions. Buddhism, in particular, became highly influential throughout Southeast Asia.

India's influence was more subtle. There is no evidence of any Indian invasion of Southeast Asia, but by around 500 CE, Indochinese sculptors were carving statues of Vishnu, an important god in the Indian Hindu religion. Inscriptions in Sanskrit started to appear on ornamental stones erected in several parts of Southeast Asia, including Vietnam, Malaysia, Borneo, and Java. Sanskrit was a ritual language that was not spoken in everyday life; it was used only by Indian priests and scholars. Everyday Indian languages, such as Tamil, had little influence on Southeast Asia, suggesting that few Indians themselves traveled to the region. The implication is that the culture of Southeast Asia came under relatively little external pressure, and when it did, it was strong enough to assimilate exotic influences rather than be subsumed by them.

Mandalas

The earliest known Southeast Asian kingdom is Funan, which was located near the southern tip of modern Vietnam. Records of Funan are sketchy, and the only firm evidence of its existence is in the records of Chinese envoys, who made an inward mission there in the third century CE to investigate its thriving sea trade. Chinese diplomatic records are also the main source of modern knowledge about other important trading kingdoms that sprang up later in the Malay Peninsula and on the islands of Sumatra and Java.

However, while kingdoms became the norm in Europe, they remained unusual in Southeast Asia, mainly because the region's contact with India had inspired a lasting political change—the adoption of *mandalas*. A mandala is effectively equivalent to a modern

from the Chinese who had dominated them for nearly a thousand years. In Java and Burma, the Sanskrit inscriptions stopped at the end of the thirteenth century CE. Thereafter, the culture of both places became identifiably national—Javanese and Burmese, respectively.

Chinese and European Incursions

The thirteenth century CE brought an influx of Chinese immigrants to Southeast Asia. The newcomers provided an important stimulus to the growth of cities in the region. Most Southeast Asian capitals, such as Angkor, were still mainly religious and ceremonial centers, with relatively few inhabitants and strictly limited economic activity. Beginning in the thirteenth century CE, however, and accelerating into the fourteenth century CE, cities in the modern sense began to form in several coastal areas of Southeast Asia.

Malacca, for example, founded on the Malay Peninsula in 1400 CE, was a thriving port. The imperial Chinese fleet docked in the city's harbor on seven occasions between 1403 and 1433 CE. At the time, the natives welcomed the opportunity for trade, but foreign interest in the region would later increase with severely damaging effects.

The Chinese, stung by their defeat by the Vietnamese in 1427 CE, renounced any expansionist ambitions in Southeast Asia. The Europeans, however, had suffered no such adverse experiences, and after the entry of the Portuguese into Malacca in 1509 CE, Westerners soon became the most destructive interlopers of all. At first, their visits aroused little local comment. Long-distance sea voyages were already unremarkable, and Asia had had limited but steady contact with the West since the time of Marco Polo (ca. 1254–1324 CE). The Southeast Asians again welcomed the economic benefits of foreign visits, but the Europeans cast covetous eyes on the wealth of the region and sought ways to exploit it.

The Spice Trade and Colonization

As early as imperial Roman times, Europeans had been eager to import spices from the East. The most important such products grew in Indonesia. Pepper was found in many of Indonesia's eighteen thousand islands, while nutmeg and cloves grew in only one small area—the **Spice Islands**, now called the Moluccas, which lay in northeastern Indonesia.

The quest for spices lay behind much of the European expansion that occurred in the sixteenth century CE. The explorer Christopher Columbus was hoping to find a route to the Spice Islands when he landed in the Americas in 1492 CE. The European demand for spices to flavor food could yield considerable riches for those who were prepared to travel to search for them.

At this time, only the Spanish in the Philippines had colonial ambitions; the aim elsewhere was simply to take as much as possible at the least expense. The Portuguese capture of Malacca in 1511 CE began a new and inauspicious chapter in Southeast Asian history, which reached its lowest point in the nineteenth century CE, when Britain, France, and Portugal took parts of Southeast Asia into their empires.

The Great Mosque of Medan is one of Indonesia's many Islamic centers. The religion began to take hold in the country in the thirteenth century CE. Today, Indonesia is home to the world's largest Muslim population.

Religious Upheaval

The period immediately prior to the start of European incursions into Southeast Asia was a time of great religious upheaval. On the mainland, both Hinduism (which was dominant in Cambodia) and Mahayana Buddhism (which had been popular among the Mon) gave way to Theravada Buddhism, a belief system that was simpler but more exclusive than its predecessor.

Meanwhile, Islam was taking hold in the region. The late thirteenth century CE saw its arrival in Sumatra and the beginning of a process of conversion. In the 1400s CE, Malacca officially adopted Islam—it was the first of the major kingdoms to do so. Thanks to its status as a major trade hub, Malacca became something of a staging ground for the further spread of the Muslim faith throughout the Southeast Asian archipelago. The arrival of the first Europeans in Indonesia initiated a familiar clash of cultures, and the region became yet another front in the continued struggle between Christendom and Islam.

The remote and enigmatic Easter Island is dotted with hundreds of stone heads. The oldest of them date to the eighth century CE.

CHAPTER TEN

Pacific Island Cultures

On the islands of the Pacific Ocean, many cultures remained untouched by the outside world for a long time. While the first civilizations of the Pacific emerged approximately thirty thousand years ago, some saw no external contact or influence until as late as the eighteenth century CE.

There are about twenty-five thousand islands scattered over an area of around 64 million square miles (165 million sq km) in the Pacific Ocean. Some of these islands are clustered together in groups; others are among the most remote places on Earth. None is more cut off than Easter Island (see sidebar, page 138), which is 1,200 miles (1,900 km) east of its closest neighbor, Pitcairn Island, and 2,200 miles (3,500 km) from the coast of Chile in South America.

Melanesia, Micronesia, and Polynesia

The islands of the Pacific are conventionally categorized into three large groups: Melanesia, Micronesia, and Polynesia. Melanesia (from the Greek *melas*, meaning "black," and *nesos*, meaning "island") is named for the predominantly dark-skinned peoples who originally inhabited New Guinea (the largest Pacific island), the Bismarck Archipelago, Fiji, Vanuatu, New Caledonia, and the Solomon Islands.

Micronesia (from the Greek for "small islands") lies mainly to the north of the equator and to the east of the Philippines. (The Philippines, although themselves a collection of islands in the

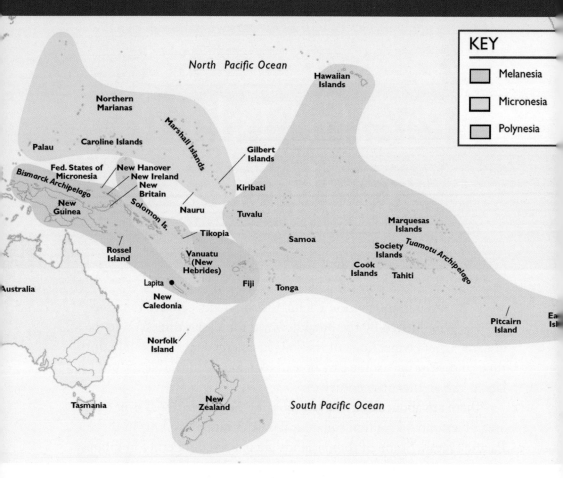

North Pacific Ocean

Hawaiian
Islands

Northern
Marianas

Marshall Islands

KEY

Melanesia

Micronesia

Polynesia

Palau

Caroline Islands

Gilbert
Islands

Fed. States of   New Hanover
Bismarck Archipelago   Micronesia   New Ireland
New
Britain

Kiribati

New
Guinea

Solomon Is.

Nauru

Tuvalu

Marquesas
Islands

Rossel
Island

Tikopia

Samoa

Society
Islands   Tuamotu Archipelago

Australia

Vanuatu
(New
Hebrides)

Cook
Islands   Tahiti

Lapita ●

Fiji

Tonga

New
Caledonia

Pitcairn
Island   Ea
Isl

Norfolk
Island

Tasmania

New
Zealand

South Pacific Ocean

Pacific Ocean, are generally treated separately from the three main groups under consideration here.) Micronesia consists of around two thousand islands, the largest and most important of which are the Northern Marianas, Palau (Belau), the Marshall Islands, Tuvalu, Kiribati, Nauru, and the Federated States of Micronesia (a republic that incorporates the Caroline Islands and has its capital at Palikir on Pohnpei Island). The smallest landfalls in Micronesia are no more than coral atolls (reefs), most of which are uninhabited.

The main islands of Polynesia (from the Greek for "many islands") are the Hawaiian Islands, New Zealand, and Easter Island. Within the triangle that they form are Samoa, Tahiti, Tonga, the Society Islands, the Tuamotu Archipelago, the Marquesas Islands, and the Cook Islands.

The islands of the Pacific Ocean are so far apart and so different in character that it is difficult to make generalizations that hold for all—or even most—of them. Another problem facing people who wish to study their cultures is that of accurate historical documentation. The islands were unknown to Europeans until the sixteenth century CE. Many of the indigenous peoples have their own records of ancient times, but their accounts—based mainly on oral tradition—are not necessarily historically accurate, and they are not always fully understood by modern scholars.

Lapita Culture and Early Migration

The first confirmed civilization in the Pacific arose around 30,000 BCE. Although it is known as the **Lapita** culture (from the site in New Caledonia where the earliest relics were unearthed in the twentieth century CE), it is thought to have originated in New Guinea, which was still joined to Australia at the time. (The two lands were later divided by sea around ten thousand years ago.) Lapita pottery reached Tasmania by around 9000 BCE and Fiji by around 1000 BCE. It was then transported by sea to Tonga, Samoa, and Micronesia. The Lapita culture had spread to eastern Polynesia by 500 BCE and to the Marquesas Islands by the second century BCE.

The pioneer migrants to the most distant parts of the Pacific are thought to have originally been Indonesians who were displaced by

This reconstructed pot is a remnant of the ancient Lapita culture.

settlers from continental Asia. The eastward migration left traces as far as Polynesia, but the only permanent settlements were in Micronesia. In all other areas, the early settlers were either driven out or exterminated by later waves of immigrants. It is assumed that the people who migrated between 100 and 1000 CE followed two routes: a southern path through New Guinea and Samoa to the archipelagoes of the central Pacific and a northern path through the Caroline and Marshall islands to the farthest reaches of Polynesia. The edges of Polynesia were the last parts of the region to be inhabited. Easter Island was reached around 400 CE, while New Zealand and the Hawaiian Islands were first settled between around 750 and 1000 CE.

Thereafter, technological development was slow throughout the region. The main reasons for that are clear; most of the islands were too far apart for the dissemination and cross-fertilization of ideas. Also, competition was minimal; despite the limited resources available to them, each society was self-sufficient. Even on individual islands, coastal communities were

Navigating the Ocean

Contact between the various Pacific island groups may have been limited, but it was not nonexistent. The most wide-ranging islanders were the Polynesians, who could, on occasion, cover distances of more than 5,000 miles (8,000 km). They undertook such journeys in canoes, some up to 100 feet (30 m) long, made from hollowed-out tree trunks. For the longer expeditions, they used a double boat—a large canoe for the rowers and a small one for the provisions. The two vessels were joined by a wooden bridge.

The rations on board were mainly breadfruit, which could stay fresh for more than a year, and coconuts, which provided both food and drink. Water was stored in bamboo casks. The Polynesians navigated by the stars, but they were also familiar with prevailing winds and ocean currents. Some kept charts of ocean currents drawn on pieces of wood.

often cut off from each other by impassable mountainous interiors; that was particularly true of New Guinea but also applied to smaller islands, such as the Hawaiian Islands, Samoa, and the Society Islands—which are all steep volcanic protrusions rising out of the sea.

It was a consequence of these limitations that, by the time the first Europeans arrived by ship, the societies of the Pacific Ocean were still Neolithic in character. The inhabitants' tools were made of stone, bone, and shell. Almost the only edible native plants were bananas, breadfruit, calabash (bottle gourds), coconuts, pineapples, taro, and yams. The one vegetable import of exotic origin was the sweet potato, which had been brought to Polynesia from South America in prehistory.

The indigenous peoples made cloth from the bark of the Asiatic paper mulberry tree and rope from the bark of the *Triumfetta semitriloba*. They had only three domesticated animals—chickens, dogs, and pigs—which had been imported from Asia. The islanders were skilled at sea fishing and navigation, but they nevertheless had only limited contact with neighboring islands; the distances between each outcrop in the ocean were generally too great to be undertaken in the islanders' tiny sailing vessels. Such subsistence cultures generally had no use for art; Lapita pottery was abandoned in Samoa and the Marquesas Islands shortly after it had been introduced.

Pacific Cultures and Languages

The ancient peoples of Melanesia were enormously diverse. However, some generalizations may safely be made. One is that they were often clearly divided between coastal and inland populations. The former traditionally had the most frequent contact with other islands, while the latter tended to remain isolated from external influences. In both areas, the main occupation was pig farming. Societies were patrilineal; each community had its own "big man," a title that was passed from father to son. Melanesians were animists; they practiced magic and worshipped totems.

In Micronesia, the early populations were concentrated by the seashore (many of the islands are too small to have interiors worthy of the name) and worked in fishing or short-haul interisland trade.

Easter Island

The first European to sight Easter Island was the Dutchman Jacob Roggeveen, who spent a single day—Easter Sunday—there in 1722 CE. In 1770 CE, the island was found again by a Spanish expedition from Peru. Four years later, James Cook "discovered" it once more. When French navigator Jean-François de Galaup landed there in 1786 CE, he became the fourth European to think that he was the first Westerner to see it.

Easter Island is famous for the gigantic stone statues—more than six hundred of them—that decorate the coast and the slopes of the extinct central volcano, Rano Raraku. The statues are human effigies and have stone platforms (ahus) on their landward sides. The oldest of them were erected between 700 and 850 CE.

There are no similar statues anywhere else in Polynesia, although there are some similarities between them and Aztec megaliths in Central America. Each statue stands between 10 and 20 feet (3–6 m) tall and weighs between 25 and 82 tons (25.4–83.3 metric tons). The indigenous peoples had no lifting apparatus and seemed, like all the other inhabitants of Polynesia, to be technologically primitive. Therefore, the Europeans were soon preoccupied with how the statues had been put into position.

The lack of firm evidence about the origin of the statues inspired numerous theories—some plausible, others preposterous. One of the most famously far-fetched theories was that of Swiss author Erich von Däniken, whose *Chariots of the Gods* proposed that the statues were installed by extraterrestrials. The book, published in 1968 CE, was an international best seller. What it failed to take into account, however, was that reenactments carried out more than a decade earlier had demonstrated that the Easter Islanders were easily capable of moving the great carvings themselves.

In contrast to Melanesia, many Micronesian societies were matrilineal; property and honorary titles were passed from generation to generation on the mother's side. Group worship was unusual; most religious observances were conducted privately within families or clans.

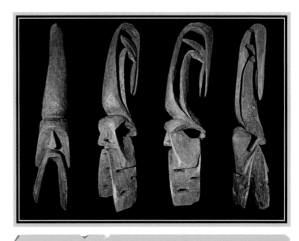

This Polynesian woodcarving of a frigate bird, shown from multiple angles, was used as the prow of a canoe.

Of the early inhabitants of the three main island groups, those of Polynesia are the easiest to summarize. Their main commercial activities were fishing and pig farming. Artistically, they were the most productive of the Pacific islanders, and they accorded their bards and sculptors the same high social recognition as their warriors and civic leaders. Polynesian mythological epics and genealogies are important sources of information about Pacific island life before the sixteenth century CE. Polynesians were also the most accomplished of the Pacific peoples at carving wood and stone. Their family structures attached almost equal value to both matriarchal and patriarchal traditions. Polynesian faith was based on mana, a spiritual quality that was believed to be invested by supernatural forces in individuals, organizations, and inanimate objects. Although the concept of mana was also familiar in Melanesia and Micronesia, it was in Polynesia (particularly among the Maoris of New Zealand) that the belief system was most fully developed.

Around 450 languages are spoken in the Pacific islands. They all belong to the Austronesian family and derive ultimately from Proto-Oceanic, a notional common ancestor that originated in Taiwan. Today, the most common Oceanic languages are Samoan and Eastern Fijian (around three hundred thousand native speakers each), followed by Kiribati, Kuanua, Maori, and Tongan (around one hundred thousand each). The total number of speakers of the modern Oceanic languages is thought to be no more than two million, which is probably the highest total in history. Still, that is an average of fewer than

4,500 speakers per language, further testament to the isolation of each small pocket of civilization.

European Exploration

The first European to reach Oceania was **Ferdinand Magellan** (ca. 1480–1521 CE), a Portuguese explorer who, having rounded Cape Horn, entered (and named) the Pacific Ocean in 1520 CE. He was followed in 1567 CE by his compatriot, Álvaro de Mendaña de Neira, who visited the Solomon Islands. In 1606 CE, Pedro Fernández de Quirós discovered the Tuamotu Archipelago, the northern Cook Islands, Tikopia, and the New Hebrides (Vanuatu). One of Quirós's shipmates, Luis Váez de Torres, later reached southeastern New Guinea. Portugal then abandoned exploration of the region because it seemed to offer little or no commercial opportunity.

The next wave of European explorers came from Holland. In 1615–1616 CE, Jakob Le Maire visited Tonga, New Ireland, and New Hanover. In 1642 CE, Abel Tasman sighted New Zealand, Tonga, some of the Fiji Islands, and New Britain. In 1722 CE, while crossing the Pacific Ocean from east to west, Jacob Roggeveen found Easter Island, the northern Society Islands, and some of the Samoan islands. He also rediscovered parts of the Tuamotu Archipelago. The Dutch then lost interest in exploring the region, for much the same reason as the Portuguese.

The British first arrived in the area in the eighteenth century CE. In 1700 CE, the pirate William Dampier sailed the Royal Navy ship under his command, HMS *Roebuck*, into New Hanover, New Britain, and New Ireland. In 1765 CE, Admiral John Byron found more of the Tuamotu Archipelago and the southern Gilbert Islands (now part of Kiribati). In 1767 CE, Samuel Wallis found Tahiti, more of the Tuamotu Archipelago, and the Society Islands. In the same year, Philip Carteret found Pitcairn Island and rediscovered the Solomon Islands.

In 1768 CE, French navigator Louis-Antoine de Bougainville sighted some of the New Hebrides and Rossel Island in the Louisiade Archipelago.

The European powers deemed the Pacific islands unworthy of colonization, due to the region's lack of exploitable resources. Published accounts of the voyages of explorers such as Dampier and

This print, from John Cleverly the Younger's *Views of the South Seas*, depicts the arrival of James Cook in Tahiti.

Bougainville were widely read with great interest, however. Inspired by these chronicles, the English sea captain James Cook set off on three separate Pacific expeditions. First, Cook journeyed to Tahiti in 1769 CE, where he took advantage of a rare opportunity to observe the transit of Venus—the passage of the planet directly between the Sun and Earth. This was an important scientific endeavor, as an accurate timing of the transit could lead to a more precise calculation of the astronomical unit, or the distance between Earth and the Sun.

Cook was also searching for the fabled—and, ultimately, fictional—antipodean continent known as Southland. Instead, while sailing the South Pacific, he discovered new islands in the already partially explored island groups of Fiji, New Caledonia, and the New Hebrides, as well as in the Tuamotu Archipelago and the Marquesas Islands. Additionally, Cook found a group of islands previously known as Kuki Airani to the Maori people. They were subsequently renamed as the eponymous Cook Islands.

On his final expedition, begun in 1776 CE, Cook focused on the North Pacific, where he discovered Christmas Island and some new islands in Tonga and Hawaii. He died while still on the voyage, in Hawaii, on February 14, 1779 CE.

CHRONOLOGY

ca. 38,000 BCE
Humans first begin to inhabit Southeast Asia.

ca. 30,000 BCE
Lapita culture develops in New Guinea.

ca. 7500 BCE
Jomon period begins in Japan.

ca. 6000 BCE
First farmers present in southern Asia.

ca. 5000 BCE
Emergence of Yang-shao culture in China.

ca. 2600 BCE
Earliest Indus Valley civilization develops.

ca. 2200 BCE
Establishment of first Chinese dynasty, the Xia.

ca. 1766 BCE
Shang dynasty begins rule of Yellow River Valley.

ca. 1500 BCE
Aryans enter India from central Asia. First Vedas composed.

ca. 1200 BCE
Vedas first written down.

ca. 1100 BCE
Iron Age begins in India.

ca. 1050 BCE
Shang dynasty in China ousted by Zhou.

ca. 1000 BCE
Caste system emerges in India.

ca. 900 BCE
First Brahmanas composed as glosses to Vedas.

ca. 800 BCE
Early Upanishads appended to Vedas.

ca. 570 BCE
Lao-tzu born.

ca. 563 BCE
Siddharta Gautama born.

551 BCE
Kongqiu (known in West as Confucius) born.

ca. 528 BCE
Siddharta becomes the Buddha.

ca. 500 BCE
Magadha becomes leading state in India. People of Dong Son culture begin to make bronze drums in Vietnam.

ca. 490 BCE
Lao-tzu dies.

ca. 483 BCE
The Buddha dies.

479 BCE
Confucius dies.

ca. 475 BCE
Period of the Warring States begins in China.

ca. 383 BCE
Buddhists split into two factions at council in Vaishali.

ca. 371 BCE
Confucian philosopher Mencius born.

321 BCE
Mauryan period begins in Magadha.

268 BCE
Ashoka becomes emperor of India. He soon converts to Buddhism.

ca. 250 BCE
Jomon period ends in Japan; Yayoi period begins. Theravada Buddhism established in Ceylon.

221 BCE
Period of the Warring States ends. Shi Huang Di becomes first emperor of China at start of Qin dynasty.

213 BCE
Qin adopt legalism as state philosophy. Shi Huang Di orders burning of books.

206 BCE
Rebellion by Liu Bang leads to downfall of Qin dynasty and marks beginning of Han period.

204 BCE
Great Wall of China completed.

ca. 200 BCE
Composition of *Laws of Manu*, early Hindu scripture.

185 BCE
Mauryan Empire ends in India; Shunga dynasty begins.

ca. 140 BCE
Wu Ti becomes emperor of China; during his reign, Han dynasty reaches height of its power.

136 BCE
Han dynasty officially adopts Confucianism as Chinese state philosophy.

ca. 110 BCE
China subjugates northern Vietnam, which becomes province of Annam.

ca. 100 BCE
First Chinese historical work, *Shih-chi*, written.

9 CE
Wang Mang, a usurper, establishes short-lived Xin dynasty in China.

23 CE
Xin dynasty comes to end.

ca. 100 CE
Inhabitants of Indonesia begin to migrate eastward and settle in Micronesia and Polynesia.

220 CE
Second Han period ends in China.

ca. 320 CE
Gupta dynasty begins in India.

ca. 400 CE
Hinduism develops into approximately modern form. First settlers arrive on Easter Island.

ca. 500 CE
Buddhism established in China and Thailand.

ca. 550 CE
Buddhism imported to Japan from Korea.

618 CE
Tang period begins in China after overthrow of Sui dynasty.

ca. 675 CE
Srivijaya kingdom starts to dominate maritime trade around Malay Archipelago in Southeast Asia.

702 CE
Japan adopts state system similar to that of China as result of Taika Reforms.

710 CE
Heijo becomes Japan's first fixed capital.

711 CE
Arab forces attack Sind.

ca. 750 CE
Pala dynasty begins in Bengal.

ca. 800 CE
Khmer state begins to flourish in present-day Cambodia.

ca. 1010 CE
The Tale of Genji written in Japan.

1024 CE
Muslim troops destroy Hindu temple at Somnath.

ca. 1100 CE
Islamic conquest of northern India marginalizes region's Buddhists. Zen Buddhism established in Japan. In Cambodia, work begins on Khmer temple of Angkor Wat.

1192 CE
Minamoto Yoritomo becomes shogun (military ruler) of Japan.

1206 CE
Mamluk dynasty begins rule from Delhi.

1215 CE
Genghis Khan captures Yenking (modern Beijing).

1281 CE
Typhoon destroys Mongol force during attempted invasion of Japan.

1290 CE
Mamluk dynasty ends in Egypt.

1368 CE
Ming dynasty established in China.

1398 CE
Mongols under leadership of Tamerlane attack Delhi.

ca. 1450 CE
Malacca becomes first Southeast Asian state to adopt Islam.

1511 CE
Portuguese capture Malacca.

1520 CE
Portuguese explorer Ferdinand Magellan becomes first European to enter Pacific Ocean.

1526 CE
Delhi Sultanate ends.

1549 CE
Jesuit missionary Francis Xavier arrives in Japan; arrival leads to establishment of Christianity there.

1642 CE
Abel Tasman sights New Zealand.

1687 CE
Mughals conquer Golconda.

1722 CE
Jacob Roggeveen discovers Easter Island, so named because he arrived there on Easter Sunday.

1769 CE
James Cook arrives in Tahiti.

GLOSSARY

Amaterasu Japanese sun goddess from whom the imperial family claims direct descent.

Angkor Wat A famous Khmer temple complex in present-day Cambodia, built around 1100 CE.

Aryans Prehistoric inhabitants of Iran and northern India.

avatar In Hinduism, the incarnation of a deity in human or animal form; for example, any of the ten manifestations of the god Vishnu.

Brahma The creator, one of the three principle Hindu gods.

Buddhism Religion founded by Siddharta Gautama, called the Buddha. Its goal is nirvana (release from all desire and from the cycle of life, death and rebirth). The major schools of Buddhism are Theravada and Mahayana.

Cham Austronesian-speaking carvers and temple builders who prospered until they were subdued by the Vietnamese in the fifteenth century CE.

Confucianism Chinese philosophy originated by Confucius around 500 BCE; emphasizes the importance of learning and the need for internal and external order through virtuous living and a respect for tradition.

Delhi Sultanate Principal Muslim sultanate in northern India (1206–1526 CE).

Dong Son Southeast Asian culture that emerged around 2000 BCE; named for the Vietnamese village where artifacts were first discovered.

Ezo Northern part of Japan roughly coextensive with the island of Hokkaido.

Fujiwara Family A prominent ruling family of Japan (858–1060 CE).

Great Wall of China Defensive barrier extending for 4,160 miles (6,700 km) along the country's northern and eastern frontiers; completed in 204 BCE.

Gupta Empire Dynasty that ruled much of India (ca. 320–550 CE).

Han dynasty Ruling Chinese dynasty (206 BCE–220 CE); introduced Confucianism as the state religion and required all political officials to pass examinations.

Heijo City in Nara that became Japan's first fixed capital in 710 CE.

Hinduism Predominant religion in India, originating from Brahmanism; characterized by belief in many gods, including Brahma, Shiva, and Vishnu.

Homo erectus First hominid species found outside of Africa; walked upright and used tools and fire; lived between 500,000 and 150,000 years ago.

Huns Central Asiatic people noted for horsemanship and ferocity in battle.

Jainism Religion of India that teaches a path to spiritual purity and enlightenment through a disciplined mode of life founded on nonviolence to all living creatures; founded by Vardhamana (Mahavira) around the sixth century BCE.

Jomon Period Early era of arts and crafts in Japan (ca. 7500–250 BCE).

karma In Buddhism and Hinduism, a person's acts and their consequences in a subsequent existence.

Khmer Ethnolinguistic group that emerged around 800 CE in present-day Cambodia.

Lapita Southeast Asian culture dating from around 30,000 BCE; named for the New Caledonian site where pottery was first discovered.

Long-Shan (Lung-shan) Neolithic culture of central China (ca. 2000–1850 BCE); named after the site in Shandong Province where its remains were first discovered.

Mauryan Empire Major kingdom in India (ca. 321–185 BCE) that reached the height of its power and influence during the reign of Ashoka (268–233 BCE).

Ming dynasty Chinese dynasty (1368–1644 CE) under which the empire was extended substantially in all directions.

Mongols Asian tribes of horsemen who originally came from lands to the north of China; united by Genghis Khan in 1190 CE; conquered central Asian Islamic states, China, Russia, and the Delhi Sultanate in the twelfth and thirteenth centuries CE.

Mughals Muslim dynasty that ruled India (1526–1857 CE);

founded by Babur, a descendant of Genghis Khan.

Period of the Warring States
Last period (ca. 475–221 BCE) of the Zhou (Chou) dynasty during which war was a constant fact of life, although trade, agriculture, andurbanization evolved simultaneously. Legislation and philosophy, such as Confucianism, legalism, and Taoism also developed at this time.

Qin (Ch'in) dynasty Rulers of northwestern China who took control of the whole country in 221 BCE. They established a central government and replaced the old feudal system with direct administration by officials.

samurai Member of the Japanese warrior caste that rose to power in the twelfth century CE and dominated the Japanese government until the Meiji Restoration in 1868 CE.

Shang dynasty The earliest Chinese dynasty (ca. 1766–1050 BCE) of which there are documentary records. The main part of the realm was centrally governed while autonomous vassals were allowed to control outlying areas.

Shinto Indigenous Japanese religion based on the worship of forefathers. The sun goddess, Amaterasu, the first mother, was the most prominent of the goddesses. The emperor was revered as her leading priest and her son.

Shiva Hindu god of destruction and reproduction; frequently manifests in female aspects, Parvati and Kali.

shogun Originally the title given to the chief military commander of Japan; from 1192 CE, the hereditary title of honor for the emperor; continued to exist until 1868 CE.

Silk Road Ancient overland trade route that extended for 4,000 miles (6,400 km) and linked China and the West. First used as a caravan route, the road ran from all the way from Xi'an, China to the eastern Mediterranean Sea, where goods were taken onward by boat. On westbound journeys, the principal cargo was silk; wool, gold, and silver were the main commodities carried in the opposite direction.

Song (Sung) dynasty Chinese dynasty (960–1279 CE) that established its capital at

Kaifeng in northern Henan (Honan) Province.

Spice Islands The present-day Moluccas, a group of islands to the west of New Guinea; an abundant source of cloves and nutmeg, both highly desirable in the West, and thus a popular destination for European traders, beginning in the sixteenth century CE.

Taika Reforms Period in Japan (645–702 CE) during which landownership was abolished and the power of the emperor's family was extended throughout society.

Taoism (Daoism) Chinese philosophy originated by Lao-tzu (Laozi) around 500 BCE; emphasizes inner harmony with nature and submission to the Tao (Dao; the Way).

uji Japanese clans forming a tribal society worshipping their own god. The emperor stood at the head of all clans, and political battles between clan leaders caused unrest.

Vedas The earliest sacred Hindu scriptures; four collections of sacrificial hymns taken over from oral tradition of Brahmanism and prescriptions for ritual; the *Rig Veda*, the *Sama Veda*, the *Yajur Veda*, and the *Atharva Veda*.

Vishnu Hindu god called the preserver; takes human form as Krishna.

***Wu Jing* (*Wu Ching*; *Five Classics*)** Five texts dated to the Zhou (Chou) dynasty (ca. 600–500 BCE). According to tradition, they were edited or written by Confucius.

Xia (Hsia) dynasty China's first ruling dynasty; traditionally established by Yu the Great around 2200 BCE.

Xin dynasty Short-lived Chinese dynasty (9–23 CE) founded by the usurper Wang Mang; ended during the chaos that followed a devastating change of course by the Yellow River.

Yamato A Japanese province that gave its name to the Yamato Empire, controlled by the uji (clan) of the sun goddess; made sun worship the state religion; controlled other Japanese ujis from the fifth century CE.

Yang-shao Ancient Chinese farming and hunting culture (ca. 5000–2000 BCE) that also made distinctive pottery without the use of wheels; named after the village in Henan (Honan) Province in which their relics were first discovered in the twentieth century CE.

Yayoi period Era of Japanese history that lasted from around 250 BCE to the second or third century CE; characterized by the widespread practice of pottery and weaving and by the use of metal containers for the cultivation of rice.

Yin (Yinxu) Capital of the late Shang dynasty; modern Anyang in Henan (Honan) Province. At its peak (ca. 1250–1050 BCE), the city extended for 3.6 miles (5.8 km) along the Huan River.

Yuan (Yüan) dynasty Mongol dynasty established by Kublai Khan; ruled China from 1279 to 1368 CE.

Zen Buddhism Buddhist school originally developed in China, later in Japan; blending of Mahayana Buddhism and Taoism (Daoism).

Zhou (Chou) dynasty Chinese dynasty that ousted the Shang dynasty around 1050 BCE; ruled for almost a millennium until it was succeeded by the Qin (Ch'in) dynasty in 221 BCE.

MAJOR HISTORICAL FIGURES

Ashoka Mauryan emperor who ruled between 268 and 233 BCE; contributed to the spread of Buddhism across India.

Bindusara Mauryan emperor between around 293 and 268 BCE; extended his power far into southern India; father of Ashoka.

Chandragupta Maurya Founder of the Mauryan Empire and conqueror of the Indus Valley; ruled between around 321 and 293 BCE.

Confucius (Kongqiu) (551–479 BCE) Chinese philosopher and founder of Confucianism.

Genghis Khan (ca. 1162–1227 CE) First leader to unite the Mongols, whom he led on a campaign of conquest that took in China and some Islamic empires.

Iname Japanese emperor of the Soga clan; ruled between 536 and 570 CE; early sponsor of Buddhism.

Kalidasa Indian poet and dramatist; wrote in Sanskrit. His dates are uncertain, but he probably lived during the reign of the Gupta king Chandragupta II, who ruled between 375 and 414 CE.

Kanishka King of the Kushan dynasty; ruled between around 100 and 130 CE; outstanding patron of Buddhism.

Kublai Khan Mongolian general and statesman; grandson of Genghis Khan; ruled between 1260 and 1294 CE. He conquered China and became the first emperor of its Yüan, or Mongol, dynasty.

Lao-tzu (Laozi) (ca. 570–490 BCE) Chinese philosopher whose ideas are recorded in the Tao Te Ching (Dao De Jing; Classic of the Way and Its Virtue).

Liu Bang (Liu Pang) Army officer of non-aristocratic birth who proclaimed the Han dynasty in 206 BCE.

Magellan, Ferdinand (1480–1521 CE) Portuguese navigator who began the first circumnavigation of the world.

Mencius (Mengzi) (ca. 371–289 BCE) Early Chinese philosopher who developed orthodox Confucianism.

Minamoto Yoritomo Shogun ruler of Japan between 1192 and 1199 CE.

Muhammad ibn Tughluq
Sultan who briefly extended the rule of the Delhi Sultanate of northern India over most of the subcontinent; ruled between 1325 and 1351 CE.

Shi Huang Di (Shi Huang Ti)
Regional ruler who declared himself emperor of China and founded the Qin (Ch'in) dynasty; emperor between 221 and 210 BCE.

Siddharta Gautama (ca. 563–483 BCE) Nepalese holy man and teacher; founder of Buddhism.

Sima Yan (Ssu-ma Yen) Emperor of China; seized the throne in 265 CE, establishing the Jin (Ching) dynasty; reunited the north and south of the country by 280 CE. The dynasty remained stable until 290 CE.

Tamerlane (Timur the Lame)
Mongolian ruler between around 1369 and 1405 CE; subjected the Mongols in the west; conquered territory in Persia, India, Syria; spread Islam.

Vima Kadphises Kushan emperor who conquered the Indus Valley and much of the Gangetic Plain; ruled between around 75 and 100 CE.

Wang Mang Government official who overthrew the Han dynasty and founded the short-lived Xin dynasty; ruled between 9 and 23 CE.

Xavier, Francis (1506–1552 CE) First Jesuit missionary to establish Christianity in Japan.

Zhao Kuangyin (Chao K'uang-yin) Chinese general who seized the throne in 960 CE and declared himself the first Song (Sung) emperor.

FOR FURTHER INFORMATION

BOOKS

Bhaskarananda, Swami. *The Essentials of Hinduism: A Comprehensive Overview of the World's Oldest Religion*. Seattle, WA: Viveka Press, 2002.

Deedrick, Tami. *Khmer Empire*. Austin, TX: Raintree Steck-Vaugn, 2002.

Eaton, Richard M. *India's Islamic Traditions, 711–1750*. New Delhi, India: Oxford University Press, 2003.

Gascoigne, Bamber. *The Dynasties of China: A History*. New York: Running Press, 2003.

Kirch, Patrick Vinton. *The Lapita Peoples: Ancestors of the Oceanic World*. Cambridge, MA: Wiley-Blackwell, 1997.

Mason, R. H. P. *A History of Japan*. Rev. Ed. New York: Tuttle Publishing, 1997.

Possehl, Gregory L. *The Indus Civilization: A Contemporary Perspective*. Walnut Creek, CA: AltaMira Press, 2002.

Smith, Huston. *Buddhism: A Concise Introduction*. New York: HarperOne, 2003.

WEBSITES

Mongols
afe.easia.columbia.edu/mongols

Religion
www.bbc.co.uk/religion/religions

Sacred Text Archive
www.sacred-texts.com

UNESCO World Heritage Center
whc.unesco.org

INDEX

Page numbers in **boldface** are illustrations. Entries in **boldface** are glossary terms.

Abhijnanasakuntala (*Recognition of Sakuntala*), 111
Advaita Vedanta, 113
Agni, 81, 83
Ajanta, 109
Amaterasu, 49, 53
Amidism (Pure Land Doctrine), 105
anatman (no soul), 98
Angkor Wat, 125, 126, 128
Aranyakas, 79
Arjuna, 89, 111
Aryans, 63–69, **65, 67,** 77–80, 91–92
Ashikaga family, 58–59
Ashoka, 70–73, **72,** 103, 107, 110
ashramas, 87
ashwamedha yajna, 108
Atharva Veda, 67, 79, 81
atman (self), 81, 113
Ava dynasty, 127
Avatamsaka (*Garland*), 102
avatars, 85–86

Aybak, Qutb-ud-Din, 116, 118
Ayurveda, 69
Ayutthaya dynasty, 127

Babur, 117, **117**
Bahmani Sultanate, 118–119
Bali, 85, 114
Battle of Panipat, 118
Bhagavad Gita, 89
Bhairava, 88
Bindusara, 70
bodhisattva, 30, 128
Borneo, 114, **122**
Borobudur, 114, 128
Bougainville, Louis-Antoine de, 140–141
Brahma, 82–84, **84,** 88, 93–94
brahmachari (student), 87
brahman, 81–82, 113
Brahmanas, 79
brahmins, 65, **65,** 67
Brihadaranyaka, 82
Brihadishvara Temple, **112,** 113
Buddhism
  dharma (right social behavior), 87, 94–95
  Diamond Sutra, **43**
  Eightfold Path, 95, 102

  Four Noble Truths, 93–95
  impermanence (*abutya*), 95–98, **104**
  importation into China, 27, 30
  India, 71–75
Jainism, 68, 93
karma, 98
Kublai Khan, 44–45
Mahasanghikas, 101
Mahayana, 30, 101–105
Middle Way, 95
monastic life (sanghas), 99–100
nirvana, 99
  overview, 91–92, 105
  sects, 100–104
Shinto, 49–51
Skandhas, 95–98
Southeast Asia, 128, 131
  spread of, 103–105, 114
Sthaviras (Theravadins), 101–102, 131
Tang dynasty, 40, 42
Tantric (Vajrayana), 104
temples, 39, 73, **101, 125,** 126, 128
Zen, 103–104
Burma (Myanmar), 114, 121, **122,** 127

Cai Lun (Ts'ai Lun), 38
Cambodia, 114, 121–
    122, **122**, 124–129
Carteret, Philip, 140
caste system, 64–67, **65**
Ceylon (Sri Lanka),
    74, 101, 112
chakravartin, 107–108
Chalukya dynasty,
    114–115
Cham, 127
Chandragupta I, 107
Chandragupta II, 108
**Chandragupta
    Maurya**, 68–70
China
    agriculture, 5–8, 10
    army, 10, 14, 41
    balance, duty
        concepts, 28
    book burning, 14
    Bronze Age, 7
    burial customs, 8–9,
        11, 14–16
    conscription, 14
    currency, 11
    education, 20–21,
        31, 34, 39
    five basic human
        relationships, 21
    fortune-telling,
        divination, 7–8,
        22–23
    government,
        centralization of,
        13–14, 20
    houses, 6

Iron Age, 12
jade carving, 7
nobility (quality),
    21
pottery, 6–7
prehistoric people, 5
reading, writing, 8,
    11, 14, 38, 40–41
religion, 8, 11, 42
rice production, 15
sacrifice, 8
social order, 10, 34
Southeast Asia,
    influences on,
    124, 129
stone tools, 6–7
taxation, 12–13,
    35–36, 41
trade in, 37–38, 40
walls, 10
Chola dynasty, **112**,
    112–113
Columbus,
    Christopher, 130
Confucianism, 12,
    20–22, 25, 28–31,
    34, 40, 50
Confucius (Konqui),
    12, **18**, 19–22, 27, 34
Cook, James, 141

Da Xue (*Ta Hsüeh*;
    Great Learning), 23
Dai Viet dynasty, 127
Dalai Lama, 105
dalits (untouchables),
    65, 66

Dampier, William,
    140
Delhi Sultanate, 110,
    116–118
devaputra (son of
    god), 75
dharma (right social
    behavior), 87,
    94–95
Diamond Sutra, **43**
Dong Son
    civilization, 123
dukkha (suffering),
    94–98
Durga, 89, 109
Dyaus Pitar, 80

Easter Island, **132**,
    138
Egypt, 61–62
Eightfold Path, 95,
    102
Europeans, 9, 129–
    131, 137, 140–141

*Five Classics—Classic
    of Rites*, 23
Five Pecks of Rice
    Society, 38
Four Noble Truths,
    93–95
Fujiwara family,
    53–54

Gandhi, Mohandas, 66
Ganesh, 89
Gaozu, 39–40

Gautama, Siddharta, 30, 68, 71, 91–98
Genghis Khan, 44, **45,** 57
Genji monogatari (The Tale of Genji), 54, **54**
gopis, 86
Grand Canal, 39, **40**
Great Mosque of Medan, **130**
Great Renunciation, 96, **97**
Great Wall of China, 13, 14, 44
grihastha (householder), 87
Gupta, Samudra, 107–108
Gupta, Skanda, 109–110
Gupta Empire, 107–109, **108**

Han dynasty
Confucianism under, 29–31, 34
establishment, reign of, 16, 33
expansion of, 33–36
factional struggles, 37
legacy, 38
rebellions, 37–38
taxation, 35–36
Han Fei (Han-fei-tzu), 29
Harappa, **60,** 62–63, 78

Harijan (Children of God), 66
Heiji Disturbance, 55
Heijo, 53
Hinduism
ashramas, 87
avatars, 85–86
Brahma, 82–84, **84,** 88, 93–94
dieties, Western counterparts to, 80
goddesses, **88,** 88–89, 109
karma, 81–82
Mahabharata, 84–86, 89, 111
overview, 68, 75, 77
Ramayana, 84–86, 89
reincarnation, 81–82
Shakti/Devi, 88
Shiva, 62, 78, 82–83, 86–88, **87**
Southeast Asia, 128, 131
spread of, 114
trimurti (three divine forms), 82–83
unity in multiplicity, 81–82
Upanishads, 79, 81–82, 87, 91–92
Vedas, 67–68, 77–82, 87
Vedic creation myths, 80–81

Vishnu, 82–86, **85,** 88, 124
Hiranyakashipu, 85
Hiranyaksha, 85
Huang He (Yellow River), 15, 36
Huns, 35

I Ching (Yi Jing; Book of Changes), 23, 30
ibn Qasim, Muhammad, 115
impermanence (*abutya*), 95–98, **104**
Iname, 51
India
art, temples in, 109–112
Aryans, 63–69, **65, 67,** 69, 77–80, 91–92
Bahmani Sultanate, 118–119
Buddhism, 71–75
caste system, 64–67, **65**
Chalukya dynasty, 114–115
city, town structure, 62–63, 68
dalits (untouchables), **65,** 66
Delhi Sultanate, 110, 116–118
early civilization, 61–63, **63**

Ganges civilization,
  67–68
Gupta Empire,
  107–109, **108**
Hinduism (see
  Hinduism)
Indus Valley, 61–63,
  77–80, **78**
Islam, 115–119
Jainism, 68, 93
Kushan Empire,
  74–75
literature, 109, 111
mathematics, 69
Mauryan Empire,
  68–74, **70**, 110–
  111
medicine, 69
Mughals, 71–72,
  117, 119
Nanda dynasty, 68
overview, 61
pottery, 63, 68
reading, writing, 62
regional kingdoms,
  110
religion, 62, **63**, 65,
  68, 71–75, 77,
  107–109
sacrifice in, 107–109
Southeast Asia,
  influences on,
  124, 128
southern kingdoms,
  110–114
taboos (prohibitions),
  66–67

trade, 61–62, 74–75
White Huns
  (Hepthalites),
  109–110
Indonesia, **122**,
  128–130, **130**
Indra, 83
Iraq, 115
Islam, 110, 115–119

Jainism, 68, 93
janapadas, 68
Japan
  agriculture, 47
  burial customs, 49
  Chinese influences,
    14, 56
  Confucianism, 50
  emperor as divine
    being, 48–49
  Empire, birth of,
    48–49
  Ezo war, 53
  freemen, 51–52
  Fujiwara family,
    53–54
  Iron Age, 48
  land privatization,
    53–54
  language, 56
  literature, 48, 54
  map, **52**
  Mongols, 57–58, **58**
  Onin War, 58–59
  overview, 47
  Period of the
    Warring States, 59

pottery, 48
prehistoric, 47–48
religion, 49–51, 53
samurai, 55–57
Shinto (Buddhism),
  49–51
shogun, 55–57
slaves, 52
social order, 51–53
Soga clan, 51
state system, 51–52
Taika Reforms,
  51–53
Tang dynasty
  influence, 40
taxation, 52
Yamato period, 49–51
Zen Buddhism,
  103–104
Java, 114, **122**, 127
Jayavarman IV, VII,
  128
Jin dynasty, 38, 44
Jomon period, 48

Kadphises, Vima, 74
Kali, **88**, 89
Kalidasa, 109, 111
Kalinga, 73–74, 103
Kalki, 85–86
kalpas, 84
Kammu, 53
Kamsa, 86
Kanishka, 74
karma, 81–82, 98
kevala jnana, 93
Khalji dynasty, 118

Khan-balik (Cambaluc), 44–45
Khitan Mongol Liao dynasty, 42–43
Khmer empire, 122, 124–129
Kojiki, 48
Kokin-shu, 54
Korea, 35
Krishna, 86, 88
kshatriyas, 65, **65**, 67
Kublai Khan, 44–45, 57
Kumarasambhava, 111
Kurma, 85
Kyoto, Japan, 58

Lankavatara, 102
Lao-tzu (Laozi), 12, 19, 22–25, **26**, 27, 30, 40
Laos, 121, **122**
Lapita culture, **135**, 135–137
Laws of Manu, 83
Le dynasty, 127
Le Maire, Jakob, 140
legalism, 13–14, 16, 28–31
Li Ji (Li Chi; Classic of Rites), 23
Li Si (Li Ssu), 29
Lin Jing (Chun Qiu), 23
lingam, 88, 113
Liu Bang (Liu Pang), 16, 29, **32**, 33

Lodhi, Bahlul Khan, 118
Lodhi, Ibrahim, 117
Lodhi dynasty, 117–118
Longshan (Lung-shan) culture, 6–7
Loyang, 10
Lu province, 23
Lun Yu (Sayings of Confucius), 20–21, 23

Magadha, 68
Magellan, Ferdinand, 140
Mahabalipuram (Mamallapuram), 111–112
Mahabharata, 84–86, 89, 111
mahajanapadas, 68
maharajadhiraja, 107
Mahavira, 93
mahayugas, 84
Mahendra, 103
Mahendravarman I, 111
Mahmud of Ghazni, 115–116
Majapahit dynasty, 127
Makura-no-soshi, 54
Malacca, **122**, 129
Malaysia, **122**
Mamluk dynasty, 116, 118
Manchuria, 35, 40, 42

mandalas, **104**, 124–127
Manu, 85
Matsya, 85
Mauryan Empire, 68–74, **70**, 110–111
Meghaduta, 111
Mehrgarh, 61
Melanesia, 133–135, **134**
Mencius (Mengzi), 23, **25**, 25–28
Meng Zi (Meng-tzu; Mencius), 23
Mesopotamia, 61–62
Micronesia, 133–139, **134**
Middle Way, 95
Ming dynasty, 45
Mitra, Mithra, 80
Mohenjo-Daro, 62–63, 78
moksha (release), 82, 87
Mon, 127
Mongolia, 42
Mongols, 44–45, 57–58, **58**
Mughals, 71–72, **117**, 119

Nanda dynasty, 68
Narasimha, 85
Narasimhavarman I, 111
New Guinea, **134**, 135–137

Nihon shoki (*Chronicles of Japan*), 48

Onin War, 58–59

Pacific Islands, 133–141, **134–135**
Pallava dynasty, 111–112
Pandyas dynasty, 113–114
paramabhagavata, 109
Parashurama, 85
Parvati, 88–89
Pataliputra, 73
Period of the Warring States, 12, 58, 59
Phillipines, 121, **122**, 130
Polo, Marco, 129
Polynesia, 133–136, **134**, 138–139, **139**
Prajapati, Prajapati Brahma, 83
Prajnaparamita (*Perfection of Wisdom*), 102
pratityasamutpada, 98
Pulakesin I, 114
Pulakesin II, 114
Purusha, 65, 80–81
Pythagorean theorem, 69

Qin dynasty, 12–16, 28–31, 33–34
Qutb Minar, 116

Radha, 86, 88
Raghuvamsa (*The Dynasty of Raghu*), 111
Rajaraja I, 113
Rama, 86, 89
Ramayana, 84–86, 89
reincarnation, 81–82
Rig Veda, 65, 79–83
ritsuryo system, 51–52
Roggeveen, Jacob, 138, 140
Roman Empire, 38, 75, 80
Rudra, 83

Sama Veda, 79, 81
Samhitas, 79
samurai, 55–57
Sanatana Dharma (Eternal Law), 77
Sanskrit, 124
Sarasvati, 84, 88
Satavahana dynasty, 110–111
Seleucos, 70
Sengoku period, 59
Shandong (Shantung), 37, 44
Shang Di (Shang Ti), 8
Shang dynasty, 7–8
Shang Yang, 13
Shankara, 113
Shanxi (Shan-hsi) Province, 6
Shapur I, 74

Shi Huang Di (Shi HuangTi), 12–16
Shi-ji (*Shih-chi; Records of the Grand Historian*), 22, 38
Shi Jing (*Shih Ching; Classic of Poetry*), 23
Shikibu, Murasaki, 48
Shinto (Buddhism), 49–51
Shiva, 62, 78, 82–83, 86–88, **87**
shogun, 55–57
Shu dynasty, 38
Shu Jing (*Shu Ching; Classic of History*), 23
shudras, 65, **65**, 67
Si Shu (*Ssu Shu; Four Books*), 23
Silk Road, 37–38, 114
Sima Qian (Ssu-ma Ch'ien), 22
Sima Yan (Ssu-ma Yen), 38
Sino-Khitan empire, 42
Skandhas, 95–98
Song (Sung) dynasty, 42–45
Southeast Asia, 121–131, **122**
Spice Islands, 129–130
Srivijaya empire, 122, 124–129
stupas, 73, **101**, 102
Sui dynasty, 39
Sulbasutras, 69
Sumatra, 114, 121, **122**

Takauji, 58
Tamerlane (Timur the Lame), 117–118
Tang dynasty, 39–42, **41**, 51
Tao Te Ching (Dao De Jing), 22–24, 30
Taoism (Daoism), 12, 21–25, 30, 40
taxation, 12–13, 35–36, 41, 52
terra-cotta warriors, **17**
Thailand, 121, **122**, 127
Three Doctrines, 30. *see also* **Buddhism; Confucianism; Taoism (Daoism)**
Three Kingdoms, 38–39
Tughluq, Ghiyath-al-Din, 118
Tughluq, Muhammad ibn, 117–118
Tumulus (Tomb) period, 49–51

untouchables (*dalits*), 65, 66
Upanishads, 79, 81–82, 87, 91–92
Usas, 80
Uyghurs, 9

vaishyas, 65, **65**, 67
Vamana, 85
vanaprastha (hermit), 87
Varaha, 85

Vardhamana, 93
varna, 64
Varuna, 80
Vedanta philosophy, 113
Vedas, 67–68, 77–82, 87
Vedic creation myths, 80–81
Vietnam, 35, 40, 121, 127–129
Vijaya, 74
Vishnu, 82–86, **85**, 88, 124
Vishnu Padmanabha, 83
Vishnuvardhana, Kubja, 114–115
Visvakarman (Maker of All), 80
Vsaya, 89

Wallis, Samuel, 140
Wang Mang, 36
White Huns (Hepthalites), 109–110
Wu Ding (Wu Ting), 11
Wu dynasty, 38
Wu Jing (Wu Ching; Five Classics), 23, 31
Wu Ti, 34–36, 38

Xavier, Francis, 59
Xi Xia (Hsi Hsia), 43
Xia (Hsia) dynasty, 7

Xin (Hsin) dynasty, 36
Xinjiang mummies, 9
Xunzi (Hsün-tzu), 29, 34

Yajur Veda, 79, 81
Yamato, 49
Yang Jian (Yang Chien), 39
Yang-shao culture, 6–7
Yayoi period, 48–49
Yellow Turbans, 37
Yenking (Beijing), 44
Yijing (I-tsing), 114
Yin (Yinxu), 7, 11
Yoritomo, Minamoto, 55–57
Yuan Hong (Yüan Hung, Red River), 14
Yuan (Yüan) dynasty, 45

Zen Buddhism, 103–104
Zhao Kuangyin (Chao K'uang-yin), 42–43
Zhou (Chou) dynasty, 8–12, 19–23, 27
Zhuangzi (Chuang-tzu), 27
Zong Yong (Chung Yung; The Doctrine of the Mean), 23
Zoroastrianism, 80